TILLAMOOK BURN COUNTRY

books by Ellis Lucia:

Tillamook Burn Country
The Big Woods
*Owyhee Trails**
Mr. Football
This Land Around Us
The Saga of Ben Holladay
Klondike Kate
Tough Men, Tough Country
Head Rig
Conscience of a City
The Big Blow
Don't Call It Or-e-gawn
Wild Water
Sea Wall
Cornerstone
Magic Valley
Seattle's Sisters of Providence

*Winner 1974 Western Heritage Award

included in anthologies:

Water Trails West
Trails of the Iron Horse
Legends and Tales of the Old West
Bits of Silver

TILLAMOOK BURN COUNTRY
A Pictorial History

By

Ellis Lucia

The CAXTON PRINTERS, Ltd.
Caldwell, Idaho
1984

First Printing September, 1983
Second Printing August, 1984

© 1983 by Ellis Lucia
All Rights Reserved

Library of Congress Cataloging in Publication Data

Lucia, Ellis.
  Tillamook Burn Country.

  Bibliography: p.
  Includes index.
  1. Tillamook Burn, Or., 1933. 2. Reforestation —
Oregon — History. 3. Tillamook State Forest (Or.) —
History. I. Title.
SD421.32.07L8   1983   333.75'153'0979544   83-15164

All rights reserved. No part of this work, including text and photographs, may be reproduced or transmitted in any form or by any means, electronic or mechanical, including photocopying and recording, except as may be expressly permitted by the 1976 Copyright Act or in writing from the publisher and/or author.

Printed and bound in the United States of America by
The Caxton Printers, Ltd.
Caldwell, Idaho 83605
143920

FOR ELSIE

CONTENTS

Page

ACKNOWLEDGMENTS		ix
FOREWORD		xiii
"THE TILLAMOOK BURN" BY WILLIAM STAFFORD		xvii
INTRODUCTION: SAGA OF THE TILLAMOOK BURN		xix
I.	A RICH GOOD LIFE BEFORE THE FIRE	3
II.	THE GREAT DISASTER	37
III.	AGAIN . . . AND AGAIN . . . AND AGAIN	65
IV.	THE TILLAMOOK COAL MINERS	85
V.	THE HUSKY BRANCH LINE	117
VI.	THE ANGRY SCAR	135
VII.	AMID THE RUBBLE	171
VIII.	A GIANT FOREST LAB	197
IX.	THE SPECTACULAR 'COPTER AIRLIFT	215
X.	CRIS MITCHELL'S "CLOUD GIRLS"	225
XI.	MILL ENDS AND SHADOW-CATCHINGS	237
XII.	AND THEN CAME THE KIDS	255
XIII.	AT LONG LAST	277
STATISTICS		303
BIBLIOGRAPHY		307

Cover color photos by Alfred A. Monner, fire; Curtis Nesheim, salvage logging; others by Ellis Lucia.

Cover design by Pers Crowell

ACKNOWLEDGMENTS

SO MANY, MANY PEOPLE have contributed to this project in various ways that it is difficult to know where and how to begin giving mention to them. Like the Tillamook Burn itself, this book appears to have welled up a widespread interest from good folk in many walks of life, and almost one hundred percent cooperation. As individuals or in their professional lives, they all went that extra mile to search their minds and old dust-laden attic files for items of interest.

I truly don't know where to start and can only stress that the order of these listings has nothing to do with what was done or what was submitted. The response was heartening. I am forever grateful and can only hope that the final result will live up to expectations. Many of those who helped were old friends, colleagues, and neighbors from my newspaper days in Tillamook Burn Country. I think immediately of Mrs. Mildred S. Reeher, member of that pioneer Wilson River family, who made several trips to Portland to bring things of interest and who trustingly loaned me for over a year copies of the Reeher family histories, which were exceedingly helpful in setting the scene for the devastating tragedy of 1933. Also George Hoar of Forest Grove, who not only supplied information but did some special legwork in hopes of ferreting out some needed pictures and material. Then there is Bert Pickens, a veteran Oregon logger, who brought me several important photographs by Darius Kinsey, the famed Northwest timber photographer. And Jean Spiering, who loaned me precious prints and took the time to tell me about her own thrilling adventure as a Camp Fire Girl escaping the big blowup in 1933. One could go on and on . . .

Jim Fisher, public relations director for the Oregon State Forestry Department, gave immeasureable assistance by making the department's own collection of Tillamook Burn memorabilia available, with no strings attached. The department had been collecting materials, especially photographs, for years, and many of these are included in this book. Ralph Voorhis, assistant in public relations, gave me much patient help and deserves special thanks. Others include Ed Schroeder, Frank Sargent, Bill Phelps, Bill Holtsclaw, and Ron Smith from reforestation times in northwest Oregon; and also Larry Fick and Bill Hoskins, presently with the northwest district.

I must surely give a grateful salute to Curtis Nesheim of Seattle, who was formerly in charge of fire fighting in the Tillamook Burn and was later warden in southern Oregon. Curt and I traveled many back-road miles through The Burn, and he took the time to sort out his own file of color slides from those years, which indeed helped round out the picture-story and fill in gaps in everything from salvage logging to wildlife.

Merle Pugh and Kurt Austerman of the Portland office of the U.S. Forest Service, working with William G. Hansen in Washington, D.C., uncovered many interesting photos. George Krauss, Portland press representative of the Southern Pacific, was a great help, along with Bill Robertson of the railroad's San Francisco office, in locating historicals of the Tillamook branch. George Abdill, curator of the Douglas County Museum in Roseburg and an ex-engineer on that branch, also came forward with more material. Suzanne Richards of the *Oregon Journal* did some special checking of their files, as did Gloria Jeffcott at the University of Washington library. Susan Sayles, photo librarian at the Oregon Historical Society, made some checks of unfiled prints and negatives and was helpful with her suggestions. Fred ("Fritz") Lemcke, with whom I teamed on newspaper assignments years back, also searched his old files in hopes of locating some early pictures.

Words can never express the appreciation to my friend and colleague of long standing, Allan de Lay, who always is so very willing and able on these projects. Allan supplied many pictures and made copies of the historicals displayed at Oney's Tavern at Elsie, the closest resemblance to a logging museum in northwest Oregon. Allan also printed his full file on the kickoff of the reforestation, which makes these pages far more interesting than they might otherwise have been, and uncovered other shots he'd made over the years in The Burn.

A newspaper friend of past years, Alfred A. ("Al") Monner, handled some copy work of rare photos in my home during the winter, a field in which he has some special ability that makes them better than the originals. Les Ordman, retired newsphotographer living in Tillamook, made a special check of that county's museum files. And Jim Vincent combed his negatives and those of his father, Ralph.

Because she's far more deserving than being at the end of this list, I must now say thanks many times over to my wife, Elsie, who gave her loyal support to what turned into a lengthy and sometimes frustrating endeavor, who put up with it, including the machinations from misplaced or misfiled negatives and prints, and who insisted on doing the final typing in addition to the many demands of her own career. Thanks, honey!

Ron Fahl of the Forest History Society was most kind in his suggestions and in sending along photos from their files. Bill Hagenstein, veteran Northwest timber consultant and forester, was as always most generous in his support and cooperation. William Lyda spent much time checking over the details of his company's logging operation and double-checking it with others who were there when the Gales Creek Canyon fire broke out. Jerry D. Alto helped the project along in the early stages by turning over his pictures and some taped interviews with old-timers, among them veteran forester Henry Rierson, Oney Camberg, and Art Camberg. Oney Camberg and her son, Joe, also generously gave permission to copy the photographs displayed in Oney's Tavern.

A special word must go to Larry Kemp of Sacramento for photos and materials from his book *Epitaph for the Giants*, a vivid account of the original big fire.

I am most grateful to William Stafford, Oregon's poet laureate, for use of his thoughtful poem "Tillamook Burn" in the introductory pages of this book.

From here on I'll list others in something of a token appreciation of their efforts, without any particular order or evaluation:

Hugh McKenna, Mary Anderson, Richard Bunker, Paul Alexander, Bill Grand, Claude Palmer, John E. Benneth, Carwin A. Woolley, Don Spiering, Pat Wagler, Rae L. Brooks, Estella Kemmling, Ed O'Meara, Don Stotler, Phil Herzog, Paul Hauser, Hans Running, Mrs. Alf Johannesen, Joe Bell, Jr., Joseph Pierre, John Coats, John E. Woods, staffers of the *Washington County News-Times*, and Esther at Jones Photos, Don Holm, Tom McAllister, Gov. Tom McCall, Merlin Blais, Ed Curtin, Robert W. Keeler, Washington County Historical Museum; Charlotte Filer, Pacific University; William J. Kirtland, Western Wood Products; Tom Worcester, Dick Dyer, public affairs, Fort Lewis, Washington; Barbara A. Bower, museum curator, Fort Lewis; Michael D. Sullivan, Industrial Forestry Association; Hugh McGilvra, Hugh Ackroyd, for special favors. . . . And any others. Thank you one and all.

ELLIS LUCIA

A WORD ABOUT THE PHOTO CREDITS

In an effort to reduce clutter from repetitive picture credit lines I have omitted many of my own, including only those needing special clarification, and also many of the generous submissions from the Oregon State Department of Forestry which helped round out the story. Therefore, all uncredited photographs are either my own or from my private Tillamook Burn Collection, including many by other photographers. I have — wherever possible — given the credit lines of newspaper, free-lance, and commercial photographers of the past so as to get them in the record, and also perhaps to well up some nostalgic memories of these talented and skilled people from times when photography was a highly specialized field. Some are no longer active, or even of this planet. Others, however, are quickly recognized, for even in this changing photographic world, they are out there every day, adding to this important portion of the historical record of yesteryear.

ELLIS LUCIA
Portland, Oregon

FOREWORD

THE TILLAMOOK BURN has long been a dominant interest in my writing career, and also a rich personal experience. Ever since 1940, when by chance I enrolled in Pacific University at Forest Grove, the Tillamook Burn has continued to change and stretch, destroy and heal, like some giant prehistoric dragon, exerting its influence upon the inhabitants of northwestern Oregon.

At my arrival as a college freshman I hadn't heard of The Burn nor of the unbelievably huge forest fire of 1933. Not many people talked about the disaster which had vastly changed their lives, as though they wished to lock it away in their minds. I was well aware of the streams of black logs being hauled through town by train and truck, of the many sawmills, large and small, and of the almost constant fires and smoke palls from slash burnings over the near hills to the west. As a newcomer to Oregon I remember the 1939 fire, which showered ashes and brands upon the Seaside beach where we were summering, and also the frightening glow just beyond the ridgetops. Yet it would be years before I would understand what was happening, and what would continue to happen, to this corner of Oregon.

I was told that Forest Grove was named by pioneers for the forest meeting with a grove of giant oaks. But there was no forest — and that told the story. The Tillamook was more than just another forest fire, of which there were all too many in the twenties and thirties. This one was different. Not only was its size tremendous; it wasn't a holocaust concealed in the back country. The Tillamook was up front, where all could feel the heat, smell the smoke, and share in the ugly aftermath. The long-range impact was endured in thousands of ways, directly and indirectly, in the rebuilding of lives, different social patterns, and in the economy. Some say it even changed the weather.

The effects spilled over into the fringe communities of the Tualatin and Yamhill valleys and the towns along the coast. Unfortunately, disasters often may change directions, but also may bolster things economically, socially, and even spiritually. The Burn went on the rampage at the bottom of the Great Depression, which years later caused an old logger to tell Bill Lyda, who was unjustly blamed for the original fire:

"Someone oughta erect a monument to you and your dad. We were all down and out in 1933, and you gave us more damned work than we ever heard of."

Thousands labored in logging and lumbering, and in the goods, services, and supplies. Just down the block from our newspaper office was the Vandervelden Machine Shop, where logging and sawmill gear was repaired and rebuilt. There were many such shops scattered throughout Tillamook Burn Country. On Saturdays, with their families, the loggers came to town in their red hats, cutoff tin pants, and calked boots to mingle with townsfolk, farmers, college professors, and students. It was as strange a conglomerate as you would ever hope to see, yet a colorful sight. Among them, and holding her head high, was a stocky, tough woman who had inherited a logging operation when her husband died. He may have been killed; logging was a dangerous business, and in The Burn were exceptional problems and dangers. The too-often ambulance sirens through town were a dreadful thing to hear, especially for those associated with the industry.

Oddly, Forest Grove was a "dry town" at the time, because of the university and more than twenty churches. The loggers came anyway to spend their pay, as they did in all the other fringe communities. Local men, even college professors, worked in The Burn to supplement their incomes or to pay for a college education. The salvage years and then the reforestation program were always present. A good friend clerked in a local clothing store and, although slightly built, also set chokers in the woods. A young couple, whom you will meet in these pages, established a seed cone business to help them through college. Many virile young men, hard of muscle from summers in The Burn, gave Pacific University and nearby high schools some of the toughest football teams on record. Coaches could spend more time drilling plays and less on conditioning players, who were physically ready when they reported for practice.

This is what I mean about the Tillamook Burn being a watershed, influencing the life of the region in countless ways. Hundreds of CCC boys in the thirties surged into Seaside's roller rink on weekends to blow 'er in. World War II placed Burn timber in the front lines of defense. Reforestation brought the dawn of a new era and a new spirit, accompanied by a renewed hope for home and community and also grassroots democracy as a slow, painful, and tedious way to restore this rugged land, which Stewart Holbrook described as a "great melancholy," and experts declared was beyond redemption.

The Tillamook Burn is therefore a success story, begun years before the words "ecology" and "environment" came into everyday vocabularies and were everyone's concern. I rate it as one of the great ecological success stories of the century, especially in the way it was accomplished. The Tillamook Burn is green again because thousands of people believed in something worthwhile, even though they might never live to see and enjoy the results. Drawn together by strong feelings, they became an integrated team from all walks of life — volunteers, voters, taxpayers, foresters, industrialists, business persons, the press, loggers, lumbermen, public officials, service and youth clubs, schoolchildren, teachers, parents and their offspring — not for a year but for decades, because they wanted to make a dream come true.

In putting together this pictorial history I have attempted, in a sequence, to show how all this came about and to indicate something of life during these critical decades. My focus, quite naturally, is from Forest Grove, where I lived and worked as a reporter and editor. I make no apologies; it was an excellent viewing place, for the Forest Grove area was closely attached to the old forest, the great fires, and The Burn as a dying wasteland. Much of the flow of activity converged from the hills and canyons upon this area like some great fountainhead and spillway. Two main highways merged there, as did two major railroads and many county and secondary roads that ran deep into The Burn. No community or area felt The Burn's continuing influence, directly and indirectly, even subtly, more than western Washington County. Historically, the old forest had had much to do with the settling of the region and with its welfare. Headquarters for both the private and state forestry districts were there. Washington County Judge H. D. Kerkman chaired the governor's special forestry committee to help chart the way with the Tillamook Burn. Publisher Hugh McGilvra editorialized that it was a "must." People campaigned hard, and with emotion, to get something going. It meant a lot to them, although Tillamook County would benefit the most from any future rehabilitation.

This isn't intended to be a detailed or definitive study of The Burn. It is instead a photographic record-story of people, the happenings of the years, and how they got it all together. Life for them would have been far different had there been no big fire and no wasteland. To shape the story and bring it some balance, I combed thousands of negatives and prints of my own and those of other amateur and professional photographers. The task, like turning the pages of a family album in the attic, welled up many memories of people now gone and renewed friendships of yesteryear. These were rewarding years, despite the wars, when events in forestry and the timber industry moved in new directions. I doubt that it all could occur today. There are too many hang-ups, too many rules and regulations, too much political wrestling by opportunists, and a me-first attitude, ranging from environmental impact statements to sign-carrying protesters — over what, I have no idea, but I'm certain they would be there. One wonders whether it would be possible now to field thousands of tree-planting youngsters without great risk and much red tape and legal tangles. And the cost of the entire rehabilitation program would be astronomical.

The Tillamook reforestation was rightly timed, and none too soon. Gazing at this vast, beautifully green region today, I find it difficult to accept that it was as bad as it really was. It is no wonder young people now cannot imagine it or believe that it ever happened, for the great scars are rapidly disappearing. That's really what this book is all about — to preserve for future generations what took place and how the land was brought back. More graphically than words ever could, these pictures offer hope for other devastated areas such as Mount St. Helens, and also express the desire that the lessons of the Tillamook Burn will never be forgotten.

ELLIS LUCIA
Portland, Oregon
1983

THE TILLAMOOK BURN

These mountains have heard God;
they burned for weeks. He spoke
in a tongue of flame from sawmill trash
and you can read His word down to the
    rock.

In milky rivers the steelhead
butt upstream to spawn
and find a world with depth again,
starting from stillness and water across gray
    stone.

Inland along the canyons
all night weather smokes
past the deer and the widow-makers —
trees too dead to fall till again He speaks,

Mowing the criss-cross trees and the listen-
    ing peaks.

WILLIAM STAFFORD
Oregon Poet Laureate

"The Tillamook Burn" in *Stories That Could Be True: New and Collected Poems* (1977) by William Stafford. Copyright 1958 by William Stafford. By permission of Harper & Row, Publishers, Inc.

INTRODUCTION

SAGA OF THE TILLAMOOK BURN

WHEN YOU DRIVE WEST from Portland, Oregon, to the coastal beaches these days, you pass through this nation's newest public forest. It is also the Impossible Dream come true.

What was once, and not so many years ago, a sorry wasteland of utter devastation — and the scene of one of the greatest forest fires of all time — is green again, well on the way back to the kind of lush beauty that provokes fond memories among those who grew up within the deep shadows and fragrant woodlands. Sweeping vistas of healthy Douglas firs, Port Orford cedar, and other evergreens have replaced the rubble, the deadfalls, and the thousands of black snags of yesteryear. As such, the world-known Tillmook Burn which sprawled across four counties is no more. It is now officially called the Tillamook Forest, although to thousands of us who remember the big fires, the havoc, the dead land, and the hopelessness, it will be forever called the Tillamook Burn.

High drama took place here, not only during the frightening fires but in the long road back to rebuild the badlands. The Burn became a trailblazer — a pioneer — in forestry and ecology, years before the word was on everyone's tongue. The rehabilitation of the Tillamook Burn unfolded as a grassroots effort on the part of thousands of people from many walks of life. Those who were a part of it, from forester and logger and lumberman to grade school youngster, gaze upon this magnificent new forest with a rightful sense of accomplishment and a boastful expression of pride that "we did it."

"Every time I drive through the Tillamook Burn, I can't help but feel real proud," remarked a retired forester, who once worked in The Burn and later became executive secretary for a logging organization. "It is truly one of the outstanding achievements of this century."

The 2,500-square-mile Tillamook Burn Country opened countless doors, helped shed the hang-ups of past generations, and gave strong hope for the future rehabilitation of other great disaster areas, both natural and man-made. It changed the thinking not only in forestry and lumbering circles, but within the halls of Congress and state legislatures, and beyond our borders. The Burn reforestation was the largest effort of this kind ever attempted. Even with all its problems, all its setbacks, it fulfilled the prediction of Oregon Gov. Douglas McKay when he signed the financing bonds in July 1949: that the area would become a huge forest laboratory of experimentation that would have widespread and long-range ramifications.

Yet, in the final analysis, the comeback of The Burn was the involvement of people — Oregonians — pulling together and giving generously and freely of their time, their energies, their talents, and their dollars in an incredibly cooperative effort. I've heard the remark, from those who were close to the program, that it couldn't possibly happen today — for many reasons. Sadly, I must accept this as true. The Tillamook Burn restoration, from the early beginnings after the great fire of 1933, was a sample of grassroots democracy in action that might today be looked upon as old-fashioned. When the kids planted trees, for example, loggers gave their time and funds, unions supplied food, schools provided teachers to handle the platoons, the timber industry furnished the seedlings, business people donated sums to pay for buses and gasoline, service clubs helped out, others just volunteered. All were of a single purpose: to turn the Tillamook Burn green again.

In the latter part of the nineteenth century and the first two decades of the twentieth, Oregon's northwest corner, drenched by constant coastal fogs and heavy rains, contained one of the finest forests in all the world. Much of it was Douglas fir, of tremendous size and centuries old, inspiring the British naturalist whose name these tall trees bear.

"From the summit of the Coast Range to the tidewater lines, it is simply one vast and dense forest," wrote a wandering reporter in 1902. "It is a forest area of the giant breed, with trees ranging from eight to thirty feet in circumference, and reaching upward from 150 to 300 feet."

Save for occasional adventuring mountain men, natives, and hunters, the forest was uninhabited; the prime timber and heavy undergrowth made going difficult. It was the domain of wildlife, while the crystal clear streams and rivers were alive with salmon, steelhead, and native trout.

Then, in August 1933, in the bottom of the Great Depression, this beautiful wonderland was destroyed almost overnight, much as in the eruption of Mount St. Helens almost a half a century later. In this event nature combined with man to ravage a huge region, wipe out a way of life, and drastically change things forever.

The woods had been a tinderbox from searing heat and low humidity for much of the summer. The usual coastal fogs and brief rains were virtually nonexistent. The woods were so terribly dry that two branches rubbing together in the slightest breeze might create an explosion that could not be stopped. The morning of August 14 dawned hotter and drier than any other. Before that day was out, at least two fires were raging out of control, and possibly even a third.

Just what started the fires will be forever a controversy. One fire spread in Gales Creek Canyon above Glenwood, while a second was on the rampage beyond the summit, about five miles farther west. Originally, the canyon fire was blamed on Gales Creek (Lyda) Logging Company. The legend grew that Lyda began to drag "one more log" after being told to shut down, and that friction with a downed timber sparked the great holocaust. However, testimony in later years revealed that there was a "second fire" earlier and deeper in the Coast Range. Many are the theories regarding the cause of this second fire and how it got started, but no sound evidence has surfaced beyond the fact that it did exist.

By the following morning people were fleeing for their lives as the twin fires spread out, began crowning in the treetops, leaped miles through tall timber, and showered sparks and firebrands long distances, touching off new explosions. Thousands of men and whatever equipment was available were pouring into the stricken region. There was little they could do. Forest fire fighting was primitive by present standards, mainly with shovel and ax. Flames jumped fire trails, while backfires turned upon the crews.

Ten days later, on August 24 — a day well remembered — the humidity skidded to 26 percent. An extremely dry east wind sucked up what little moisture remained, fanning small sparks to new aggressiveness. The wind carried brands into virgin timber stands that had taken centuries to grow. Flames crowned again and again, spreading for miles. Loggers, foresters, and boys in the Civilian Conservation Corps (CCC) sensed a new terror, as the few forest wardens patrolling the area ordered a full evacuation.

Suddenly the fire blew up — literally. Nobody who saw it will ever forget. The Tillamook exploded with the ferocity of an H-bomb. Aerial photographs show a mushroom cloud resembling these latter-day frightening instruments of destruction, and also the eruption of Mount St. Helens. In twenty incredible hours, this now-single holocaust rampaged over 220,000 acres, burning fine trees at an astounding rate of 600,000 board feet an hour. Along a fifteen-mile front, the fire mounted into a awesome wall of flame, exploding again and again in the tops of the four-hundred-year-old giants and creating an inferno unlike anything since the eruptions of the Pacific Northwest's volcanic peaks. Flames leaped madly from a million blast furnaces. The conflagration built upon itself, spawning its own violent updrafts which roared like a thousand hurricanes, ripping huge firs and cedars out by their roots and flinging them great distances through the air, across deep canyons and high ridges.

Three thousand fire fighters were helpless as the gigantic mushroom cloud spiraled forty thousand feet into the sky. The cloud blotted out the sun on this and succeeding days. Chickens went to roost at noon, lights came on in the villages and small towns, motorists turned on their headlights. Photographer Joe Bell grabbed his camera to record Tillamook's business district, which was fully illuminated at midday. Sparks rained, while homeowners wetted roofs with garden hoses to protect their houses. The ash fallout came down on ships five hundred miles out to sea, on the big city of Portland, and on Boise, Idaho. My neighbor, working on federal highway construction near Yellowstone Park, saw the huge cloud one thousand miles from the hell-hole devastation. Ash, firebrands, and chunks of charred timber piled several feet deep on the normally clean beaches of the Oregon coast. Adding to the horror, some idiot arsonist started another fire to the north of Wolf Creek and southwest of Vernonia, in what could be considered a classic example of human stupidity — an unfortunately common practice during the depression years to create jobs for paid fire fighters.

The uncontrolled flames reaped their angry harvest for another two weeks along a one-hundred-mile, horseshoe-shaped front spreading through four counties. Then, at long last, the welcome rains reached the stricken and charred Coast Range. The scene, when it could be reached, boggled the mind. The devastation, covering some 311,000 acres, was unbelievable. People had difficulty grasping what had actually happened. All their known world had been wiped away, replaced by millions of black, shapeless trees, charcoal deadfalls, the grotesque forms of thousands of dead animals, and a deep ash covering everything. In places the fire had been so hot that forty years later nothing would grow there. The eerie devastation — and there is nothing quite so desolate as the aftermath of a major forest fire — covered an area half the size of Rhode Island, containing more than twelve billion board feet of prime timber, enough to last for generations.

The economic and social impact of the disaster was staggering to the northwest Oregon region, to the state, and to the West Coast. It is still impossible to grasp fully. While the loss of timber and the resulting great salvage effort have been considered many times over the years, the personal suffering of the people, not to mention their emotional and economic adjustments, has never been fully examined. Americans of that time weren't nearly as socially conscious as they are today, and despite a long, close observance of the Tillamook story, I, too, plead guilty to never having given much thought to this phase of the disaster until recent years. The people with whom I lived and brushed against for many years as a newspaperman didn't talk about it much. Thinking back, I can only believe that the hurt and heartbreak ran so deep that they just didn't care to discuss the subject. I know of no school or university course, or part of a course, that considered the subject, and if there are any theses or term papers, I am unaware of them.

Hardly had the flames died and the embers cooled than timbermen and loggers launched what was one of the great salvage efforts of all time. While the flames had killed the trees, the timber was still sound within its charcoal black covering. The major threat came from wood-boring insects, which could make potential lumber worthless. Private timber interests met with local, state, and federal officials to bring about a single concerted action. The result was formation of the huge Consolidated Timber Company, a bold cooperative enterprise at a time when such things were considered sinful and bordering on communism. At the helm, as bull of the woods, was Lloyd Crosby, a cousin of the famous entertainer, who exhibited considerable imagination to blend with his years of practical experience.

Crosby wrote himself into history for this tremendous salvage effort. He moved at high speed and with good judgment to penetrate the rugged Burn Country with a network of railroads and truck roads. The hub was the prefire camp near Glenwood, expanded into a thriving logging metropolis to become known as Consolidated Camp. The only federal aid — a point in which Oregonians still take great pride — was financing of a road along the Wilson River for logging the western side of The Burn. Before removing any logs, Consolidated spent $1.5 million in railroad construction, another $800 thousand for truck roads, and $1.25 million for locomotives, cars, and other rolling stock. Loggers worked in deep ash and soot in what became the strangest logging operation ever envisioned. They emerged from a day's work blackened beyond recognition and were called "the Tillamook coal miners."

Yet soon the black logs were streaming across the Tualatin Valley floor to sawmills enroute, or to others seventy miles away along the banks of the Columbia and Willamette rivers. The salvage effort, which would go on for years, ranked as a frontrunner in achievement of American enterprise for speed and efficiency, bringing the citation known as the Army-Navy E Award toward the end of World War II. When the figures were finally tabulated, Consolidated Timber and independent gypos had salvaged more timber than the original cruise estimates. Small operators were still scrounging the little stuff in the 1950s after the replanting program was launched, slowing reforestation because they wouldn't relinquish their lands — quite yet.

This was only the initial phase in the long road back. The Burn caught fire again in 1939 and 1945 in what were major disasters, adding to the wasteland and destroying more green timber and the little trees that, in nature's own way, would a long time hence rejuvenate the forest. Between the big fires were many smaller ones. Erosion into Tillamook Bay was tremendous. More wildlife was lost, more timber was destroyed, and the region was made more unsightly than ever. This became a major factor, for Oregonians held a certain pride in the clean, green, natural beauty of their state and region.

Oregon and Washington were huge lumber-producing states; this was a leading industry. Forest fires and break-away slash fires were a yearly occurrence, generally accepted as part of the system. Most of these charcoal scars were in the backcountry, seen only by anglers, hunters, and outdoor types. The Tillamook was different. It was within fifty easy miles of Portland, the state's largest city, and was sliced by two heavily traveled highways to the beaches. All year the public saw this wasteland at close range. Kids and adults began asking the question: "Why can't something be done?"

Public meetings were fraught with discouragement and with strong opinions that it was impossible to bring back The Burn. It was too huge, too rugged, and there were continual destructive fires. A study by the U.S. Forest Service reached the same negative conclusion. A handful of individuals believed otherwise. One of them was Nelson S. Rogers, then state forester, who had grown up around Vernonia and Gales Creek, and well remembered the way it had been. Rogers wanted above all else to bring back The Burn to full productivity, knowing it to be one of the finest timber-growing regions in the world. Proposals to turn the sprawling tinderbox into rangeland were rated as ridiculous — only mountain goats could negotiate the slopes, and the land wouldn't be at its full potential.

Rogers had a workable plan, starting with experimental projects, which he took to Gov. Earl Snell. Meanwhile, a young, enthusiastic newspaper editor, who had purchased the *Washington County News-Times* at Forest Grove just ahead of the big fire, launched his own campaign to reforest The Burn. Hugh McGilvra pounded home that point, again and again. His editorials and ideas, along with those of Nels Rogers, were reprinted throughout the state, even in the big metropolitan dailies.

The Rogers plan, which he wouldn't live to see accomplished, involved fire control, more salvage logging, felling of millions of snags averaging thirty-three to the acre, construction of a vast network of fire roads and trails, building of many fire patrol lookouts, strengthening fire crews, and partitioning areas into many plantations. Rogers and many others recognized that public funds couldn't be invested in a new forest so long as the fire threat remained.

Public hearings gathered other ideas; many meetings were held in towns and even at the Owl Camp in the heart of The Burn. Still, there remained a feeling of hopelessness. Suggestions of the grasslands idea and of seeking federal help were both soundly rejected. Oregonians would do it all themselves. Finally, in 1947, the state legislature referred a constitutional amendment to the people. The public voted the money, $10.5 million, gambling their dollars on something that was still only a vague blueprint. Fire, disease, rodents, animals, the weather, and a general lack of know-how were all time bombs against its success. Yet even far corners of the state supported the project with their votes. That was how strong feelings were about The Burn.

The challenge was tossed by Nels Rogers to a quiet-speaking district forester from Roseburg who had openly criticized a lack of organization during the 1945 fire. Rogers called his hand. John Edward Schroeder was up from the ranks of logging and lumbering. He talked the cynical loggers' language and held their respect. He also demonstrated a rare ability of picking the right man for the job and for extracting from each a fierce, devoted loyalty. Later, when he was elevated to state forester (he retired in 1980), Schroeder took along many of these top aides, who continued guiding the destinies of the Tillamook Burn and all Oregon forests.

All was not clover; far from it. Schroeder arrived at Forest Grove in 1948 amid much opposition and not-too-subtle threats. Rocks were thrown at him and his aides as they explored the wasteland and its subdistricts. Much of the opposition came from friends of Cecil Kyle, former chief warden for the private protection association, and citizens of the logging communities, who didn't want the state involved in their world and took a dim view of professional foresters. Just as things were getting well under way, The Burn exploded again in what held all the potential of another big fire. This time Schroeder was ready, having organized the loggers — no easy task. The fire was held to 2,800 acres. The amazed public began realizing this was a new age in forestry and lumbering in Oregon, and certainly within the confines of The Burn. Outcries that the project was foolish and a waste of the public's money were silenced.

The sprawling, wild region unfolded into a giant forest laboratory of trial and error, where bold new ideas were attempted and milestone successes would have worldwide impact. Experimentation became the watchword. First uses of the helicopter in forestry took place in the Tillamook Burn for aerial seeding, rodent control, mapping, photography, fire patrol, and even construction of isolated lookouts. In the late 1940s, the helicopter was still an unknown quantity, but owners and pilots were willing, at great risk, to demonstrate what the machines could do.

The now-common power chain saw was developed as a workable timber tool and was needed vitally in the felling of all those snags. In the beginning, crews were actually still using the old crosscuts and springboards. Fire-fighting and road-building equipment was improved. Planting tools were made better and more efficient. Today, seedlings are virtually "shot" into the ground, free of stoop-and-bend. More public and private tree nurseries were developed. Not all these were established directly because of the Tillamook Burn, but it was the front-running Burn program that became the trailblazer, providing the initiative.

The heavy, mounting demand for seedlings and seed (in the early years the state forestry scrounged both from any available source) led to the development of healthier strains which could withstand the rigors of the Tillamook Burn topography. Foresters learned much about the relationships of weather, altitude, and soil to the successful growing of trees, for The Burn had a wide variety of challenges. This would eventually lead to development of the so-called fast-growing Superior Tree or "super-tree," seedlings in compact capsules, and tree farms, a comparatively new concept launched in 1941 in southwest Washington. The Tillamook Burn became the largest tree farm of them all.

Foresters, lumbermen, and public officials traveled from around the world to see what was happening in The Burn. Spreading out from Owl Camp, steady progress in experimentation and tree planting went on year after year. But the most heart-warming project involved Oregon volunteers, especially the school children. Each spring fleets of yellow buses hauled thousands of grade and high school youngsters and members of youth clubs to The Burn to spend a day planting trees. The volunteers came not only from nearby, but from far corners of the state.

Special tracts were set aside for these plantings. Some were dedicated as memorial forests. Other volunteers came on their own, parents and kids stopping at a forestry station to pick up a bundle of seedlings to set out amid the deadfalls. Again, it was a demonstration of how strongly people felt about The Burn. Today, thirty or more years later, those youthful planters of the 1950s have youngsters of their own continuing to plant trees. Others drive the highways, pointing out with pride "the trees mom and dad planted when we were your age."

The work went ahead, quietly and unheralded. Planting trees isn't the fodder for such headlines as the assassination of a president, wars, mass murders, and the doings of celebrities. The country has much changed since those first seedlings went into the ground when Harry Truman was in office. In those years, the Pacific Northwest had no television, no freeways, few tall buildings. Lumber was king, and the sound of steam logging trains and sawmills filled the land. Words like ecology, environment, and energy crisis were unkown. What in the world was an "environmental impact statement"? Year after year, brawny men clung to the steep slopes and crept along barren ridges. The gnarled hands of paid planters and trusties from the state penitentiary gently placed thousands of little trees into the ground. Aerial seeding couldn't do the full job. Hand-planting proved the best method, although slower and more costly. It would be years before it looked like much of anything had been accomplished, for the seedlings were well hidden by the miles of vine maple which each autumn created its own memorable show of flaming color.

By 1973, forty years after the great fire, 73 million trees had gone into the slopes, at a varying average from 175 to 335 trees per acre. In addition, 97,679 acres were aerial seeded with thirty-six tons of seed, at one-half to three-fourths pound per acre. Happily, the survival rate has been very high. The trees from early plantings began showing above the vine maple and scrub brush. Suddenly the long years of trial, error and doubt were wiped away, as if by a magic wand. The sorry old Burn was turning green again. In that same summer, then-Gov. Tom McCall gave the region a new name — the Tillamook State Forest — in special dedication ceremonies at Rogers Camp. At the same time, the neighboring Clatsop State Forest which had been rehabilitated from over-heavy logging, was also dedicated. And, McCall added, by the great fire's fiftieth anniversary in 1983, controlled logging would likely resume as part of the promise to the people that this would be a productive, self-supporting, multi-purpose forest, albeit a well-managed one. McCall's forecast was correct: the first commercial contract logging in several decades resumed in June 1983. Ken Risseeuw, Sheridan, Oregon, logging contractor, won the bid at $75 per thousand board feet. The commercial thining contract, south of Rogers Camp, was for removal of 470,000 board feet on 114 acres — a bid of $35,000, in a two-month harvest. The logs went to Willamina Lumber Co., seventy miles away. The first tree was a 35-year-old Douglas fir, 25 inches in diameter.

The long-range effort has already been paying dividends. The new forest, within an hour's drive of Oregon's most heavily populated area, is a mecca for outdoor enthusiasts. This is part of the promise. Administered from district headquarters at Forest Grove, foresters are continuing to develop hiking and motorbike trails, self-guided walking and car tours, historical areas, small stands of centuries-old trees which were skipped by the fires, picnic and camping grounds, boat-launching ramps, fishing and hunting accesses, waysides, exhibits, lakes, waterfalls, and other scenic attractions. The signs of the return of this great forest are everywhere. With trees holding back the soil from the onslaught of heavy rains, streams and rivers have cleared. The fish have come back in growing numbers. New, healthy elk herds roam the region, along with deer and smaller animals. Many varieties of birds again call this once-desolate region home. Native wild flowers festoon the trails and glades. There are places where geologists can gather artifacts. What was once a black, desolate land is again alive and beautiful.

TILLAMOOK BURN COUNTRY

Chapter One

A RICH GOOD LIFE BEFORE THE FIRE

"Please be sure to tell them how beautiful it was..."
Mildred Reeher

IN THE NORTHWESTERN corner of Oregon, prior to 1933, existed one of the most magnificent forests in all the world. It stretched along the fog- and rain-drenched slopes of the Coast Range from the Columbia River's broad mouth south beyond what is now Tillamook County.

It was primarily a forest of Douglas fir giants which had been allowed to grow unhindered for more than four centuries. Some of these Goliaths, of tremendous girth, were nearly a thousand years old. Other memorable trees — cedar, hemlock, spruce — also flourished here in grand style, although in places they were of lesser circumference because they grew in such abundance that they couldn't fully develop. Where the sun seldom shone, the timber was so thick that passage was all but impossible. Indians feared parts of these woods because of forboding haunts. Whites skirted the fringes. The land was very rugged, the slopes and ridges steep and towering, the canyons deep, the winter snows heavy, yet the giant trees clung as tenaciously to the rough, rocky terrain as they did to the flatlands.

For centuries this green paradise had been the home of millions of birds, deer, elk, bear, cougar, and smaller mammals. Gushing streams feeding sizeable rivers were choked with trout, salmon, and steelhead. Lakes and waterfalls were hidden in the mountains. The rich earth was softly carpeted with humis from decaying needles, branches, and downed timber. Huckleberry, fern, salal, and kinnikinnick grew among countless varieties of wild flowers. It was indeed a natural wonderland, silent save for the twittering birds, the constant dripping of fog and rain, and the wind rippling through the timber.

In the latter part of the nineteenth century, more people moved into the backcountry. This big woods provided a rich way of life for homesteaders and residents of the small coastal communities of Tillamook, Garibaldi, Wheeler, and Seaside. Many villages were isolated from Oregon's mainstream beyond the tall ridges. On the coast were few connecting roads; folks traveled along the beaches at low tide or on narrow foot trails high above the sea. Changes came slowly to this vast wilderness, but nobody seemed to mind. Life was good, the outdoors abundant, the air fresh, the rivers and streams sweet, game and fish plentiful.

Yet all this beauty, all this richness of a thousand years, was doomed to be wiped away in a twinkling and with staggering impact, much as Mount St. Helens did to another area half a century later. A style of life vanished, creating overnight a vast new American wasteland. The promise of many generations was gone, and life would never again be quite the same.

Photo by Ralph Gifford   Courtesy Oregon State Forestry Department (OSFD) and Oregon Historical Society

The aged coastal forest of Tillamook and Clatsop counties was so beautiful that people yet living have never forgotten it. The Douglas fir dominated the scene in sky-holding size that must have inspired the naturalist whose name it bears. Timber was so thick that travel was difficult. Portions of the region hadn't been explored, even by natives.

Courtesy OSFD

Ellis Lucia Collection

The silent giants reigned over a rich land of natural splendor. Millions of birds and animals lived here, little disturbed by man. The beauty of the woods and the clean forest floor of fern, huckleberry, and salal, and thousands of wild blooms were an indescribable sight. The trees were up to 300 feet tall. The woodsmen in these views appear dwarfed by the tremendous size.

This forest of grandeur inspired names for the communities which rimmed its edges: Forest Grove, where thick timber met a stately gathering of gnarled old oaks, Glenwood, Timber, Mist, Jewell. . . . These woods, too, must have inspired Olaus Murie, one of the nation's great naturalists and wildlife artists. Murie attended Pacific University on the edge of the big woods and was friendly with another student, Max Reeher, who grew up in a homestead family along the Wilson River.

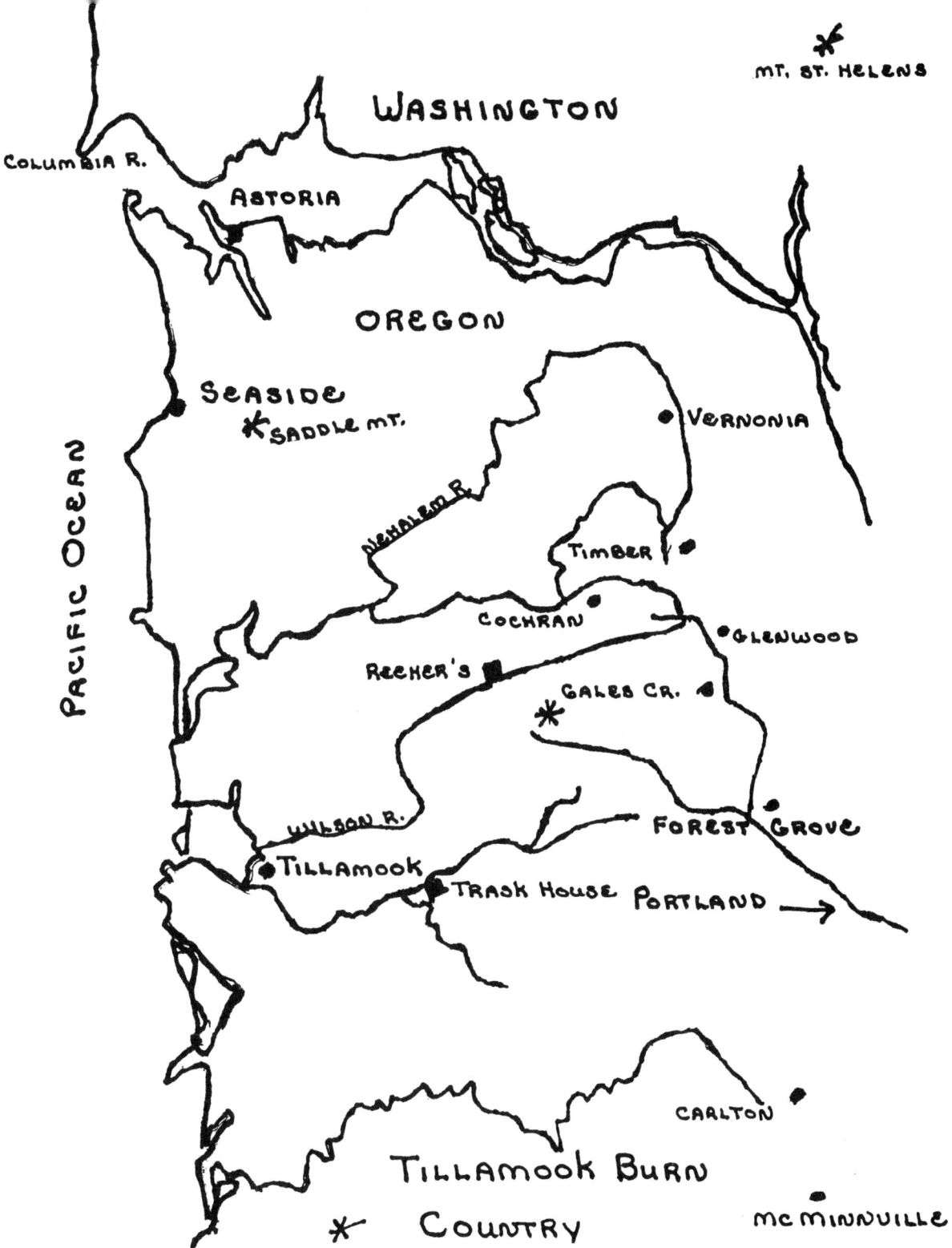

Tillamook Burn Country lies almost in the center of the northwest corner of Oregon, bounded by the Columbia River in its last swing to the sea, the Pacific Ocean, and the Tualatin and Yamhill valleys to the east. Through the center runs some of the most rugged peaks and slopes of the Coast Range.

Left: Loggers tapped only the fringes; homesteaders and outdoors people took freely of fish and game in a land of plenty. "Limits" were unheard-of. The great, clean woodland was to be enjoyed, as these young women hikers, Mrs. Maud Rockwood and Mrs. Cecil Creel, were doing as they paused by giants near Deyoe Creek.

Photo by C. Kinsey *Courtesy Oregon Historical Society*

Wildlife was abundant. The woods were alive with the chatter of thousands of birds and small animals — squirrels, chipmunks, skunks, rabbits, and other small creatures who had lived happily for centuries among the tall timber and wild flowers.

From "Sea Wall"

Deer and elk herds roamed the forest in large numbers. A monarch of all he surveys is enjoying an ocean view. Directly behind him are the western high ridges of the Coast Range.

Most homesteaders clung to the open valleys — and with good reason. The thick timber and the wild, steep, rocky land made much of it good only for growing trees. Stumpland farms like this were started, but farmers had their work cut out for them. Soil tillers viewed trees as a nuisance.

Log cabin homes were quickly built from surrounding timber. This one was occupied into the mid-twentieth century.

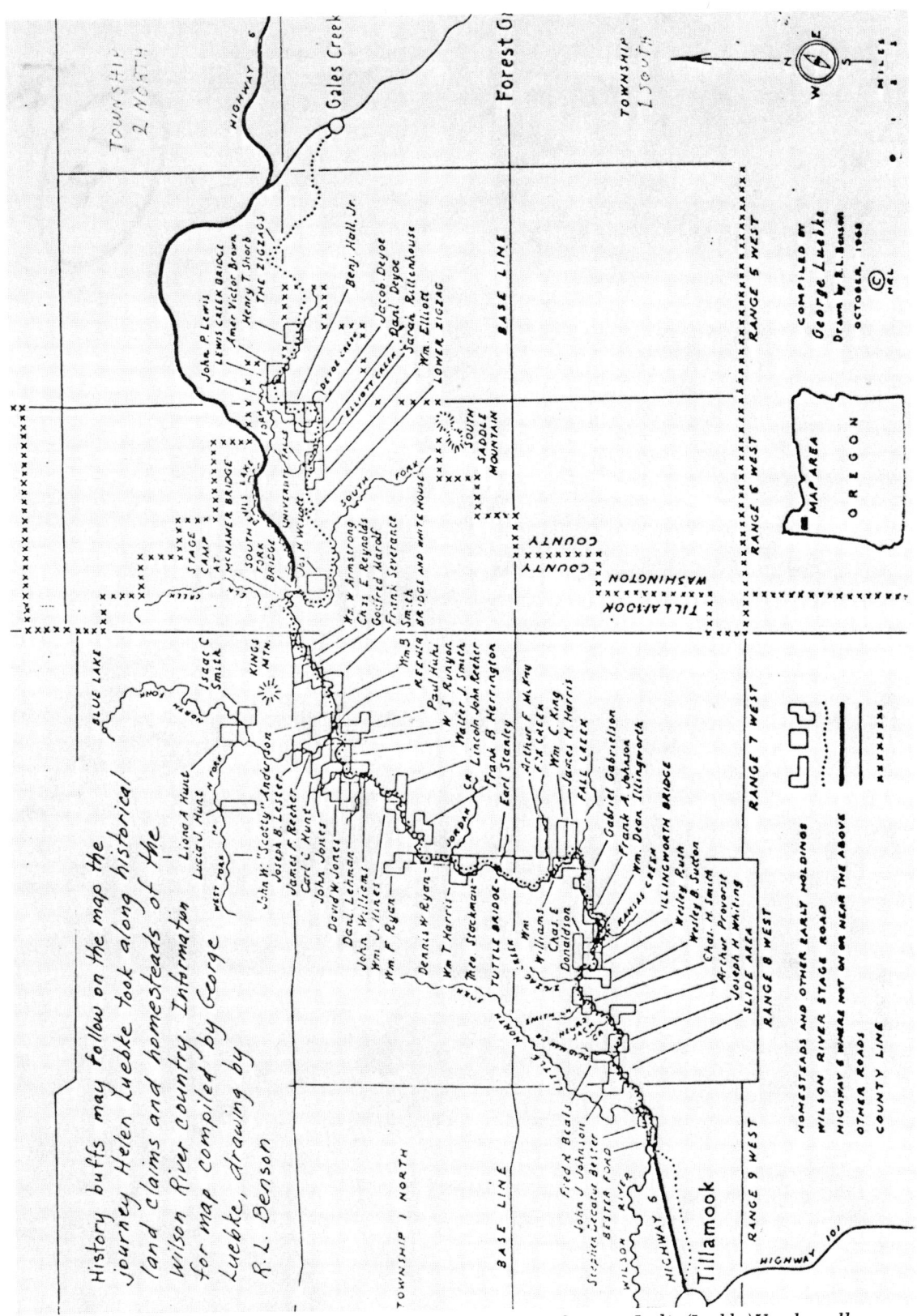

Courtesy Lydia (Luebke) Vanderwalker

More than fifty families settled on homesteads along the Wilson River east of Tillamook. This map compiled by George and Helen Reeher Luebke from extensive research gives some idea how populated the area became. The families lived an easy life for pioneers; while vegetable gardens might be small, the river was full of fish, and there was game aplenty in the forest. Later, many sold out to timber companies.

The Wilson River road connected the inland valley with the coast town of Tillamook. Fred McNamer of Glenwood established a stagecoach line (McNamer's Camp was a resting place) with regular passenger and mail service most of the year. At first it was a toll road. The old road may still be traveled today from Gales Creek.

Courtesy Oregon Historical Society

The mail stage about to leave Tillamook. This appears to be an old Concord mud wagon, minus the canvas top. The trip was beautiful, yet rugged and dangerous. Grades were steep, the canyons deep. In places, curves were so sharp passengers helped lift the stage around the turns.

Courtesy Oregon Historical Society

It wasn't easy country. Far from it! In winter, snow clogged the pass — and Tillamook had no Snowshoe Thompson to carry the mail. In the winter of 1913 mail sacks almost buried the post office, for the mail stage couldn't get through. Eventually it went via Portland by steamer.

Among the most famous landmarks of this wilderness area was the Trask House on the Trask River. It was an overnight stop for travelers and sportsmen, snubbed against the forest.

Courtesy Tillamook County Pioneer Association and Oregon Historical Society

The Trask House was a rambling frame hotel with a tall tower for viewing the surrounding landscape. In the great fire of 1933, the place was leveled.

Fish runs were fantastic in the rivers and streams of the Tillamook region. In October 1912, A. E. Williams and G. H. Toland caught one hundred big, fat Chinook and silver salmon for a total weight of two thousand pounds. They were apparently netted in the Hall Slough. Chinook sold for 3.5 cents a pound, silvers for 2.5 cents.

Courtesy Oregon Historical Society

Courtesy Mildred Reeher

The most famous wilderness center of the Tillamook region was Reeher's, along the lower Wilson River about twenty-five miles east of Tillamook. James Reeher from Kansas established a homestead on a Donation Land Claim in the late 1880s. The original house, shown here, was destroyed by fire in 1904.

The White House on the Wilson was both home and hotel, with twenty rooms to accommodate a large family and paying guests. The Reehers "took travel" as one means of pioneer survival. They also lived off the land, with game in the forest and fish in the streams. The sprawling landmark burned in 1918 in a runaway slash fire that swept across 100,000 acres. Reeher descendants still retain the homestead area.

Courtesy Mildred Reeher

Courtesy Mildred Reeher

Homestead life was isolated and rustic, but the kids had to have their book larnin'. The first school was a cabin, reached by crossing the river on logs, over a deep hole. The site was later moved closer to the road to satisfy another family.

Most of the teachers were young women, but, as in other pioneer settlements, they soon succumbed to matrimony. Oliver Curtis was the only male teacher on the Wilson. He taught at Reeher's place.

Throughout the northwest Oregon region, villages were being established, many of them connected to logging camps or sawmill communities. The Natal School, in the northern reaches of the vast Tillamook Burn country, was built in 1906 and is still standing.

The spiritual needs of homesteading pioneers weren't forgotten either, as illustrated by this beautiful little church in the timber, which members have retained with pride of continuing upkeep, even to a modern-day foundation of building blocks.

The Tillamook country had its legends, some of them well substantiated. For many decades, from pioneer times, settlers searched for the buried treasure of Neahkahnie Mountain, overlooking the sea on the western fringe of the big forest. Equally haunting was the legend of the Lost Indian Gold Mine, somewhere in the thick woods of the Tillamook. Only the natives knew its location, bringing their nuggets and dust to buy supplies at the store of Col. Thomas R. Cornelius near Forest Grove. People are still searching for both legendary treasures.

The mysterious lost treasure of Neahkahnie Mountain is one of the timeless stories of the Tillamook. A large gold cache was believed buried on the mountain by a ship's crew. Strange markings on rocks seen near the base of the mountain give credence to the legend.

Andy Phillips of Gales Creek knew well the stories of the Lost Indian Gold Mine. He spent much of his life ranging the Tillamook country looking for the supposedly rich vein. Several times he believed he had found it. Phillips collected many semiprecious stones, which he exhibited in schools and shows here to Jackie Reed and Bill Barnes.

Courtesy Oney's, at Elsie

While much of this vast forest remained wilderness, the fringes were being pushed back by outdoorsmen and loggers. It took some doing to wrestle trees the size of these firs, spruce, and cedar. Near Seaside, loggers were still using bull teams and skid roads in the late 1800s.

Horses were also used to handle hefty giants through the heavy timber stand of this rain- and fog-drenched northwest Oregon wilderness.

Courtesy Oney's, at Elsie

Despite the primitive backcountry, local logging operations joined the revolution to steam power. Increasingly, the Tillamook bustled with the sound of the steam donkey and the shrill whistle of heavy logging trains. This skidder is working a typical operation in the Seaside area. Steam mechanization, of course, also increased the danger from fire.

Courtesy Southern Pacific

Indicative, too, of growth and progress was the bold construction of a railroad to Tillamook by the Pacific Railway & Navigation Company, beginning in 1906. The mountains were tall, the canyons deep, and the building of the 167-foot-high Big Baldwin trestle was considered an engineering achievement. It ranked among the world's tallest wooden spans.

Courtesy Southern Pacific

It took several years to link Tillamook beach communities by rail to inland Oregon. Seaside had long since enjoyed train service via a water-level route down the Columbia River to Astoria. On October 9, 1911, in a heavy rain, the first passenger train left Portland for Tillamook. Regular schedules began that November.

Courtesy Douglas County Museum

The trip over the mountains was spectacular, with innumerable tunnels and high trestles. The route followed the Salmonberry River canyon to the sea, then threaded the coast to Tillamook. Wilson River people were surprised that this route was chosen over their river. (For more on the P.R.&N., see Chapter V.)

"By the sea, by the sea" was very popular with Oregonians, especially Portlanders and those of the Tualatin and Yamhill valleys. The new railroad gave access to a new environment, placing the Tillamook area in direct competition with Clatsop beaches and those across the Columbia River at Long Beach.

Quite naturally, the Clatsop area developed for tourism ahead of the coast farther south, for it had easier access down the Columbia River. Ben Holladay, the Old West's celebrated transportation king, led the way by building a palatial private hotel there in the 1870s, where he entertained lavishly. A racetrack ran in the foreground.

Top: Around the turn of the century, beach scenes like this were common and fashionable. Attire on this outing at Seaside is a far cry from today's skimpy bikinis.

Courtesy Oregon Historical Society

Right: When the United States entered World War I, a large crowd gathered at the railroad depot to send off Tillamook's own enlistees to the conflict.

Courtesy Oregon Historical Society

The region was slotted with several rivers. Log drives were another method of getting heavy timber down to the coastal mills. These loggers are trying to uncork an apparent jam along the Trask. The year is 1915. The bone white snags indicate fire had swept through here. Portions of the Tillamook country were hit by fires many times, a seemingly inevitable part of early logging.

A typical logging crew pauses beside the steam donkey, with diamond-stack logging locomotive in the background. No hard hats in those years. Calked boots, tin pants, and red felt hats were the attire of a rugged breed of men who lived with danger.

Loggers teamed with steam to wrestle the big sticks to the loading docks and then to the mills. Little did these men realize that the entire region was doomed to disaster within a few years, in one of the largest holocausts of all time.

Courtesy Oregon Historical Society

Toppling the giants was rugged work, with loggers standing on springboards and using huge crosscuts called "misery whips." It was back-breaking labor — and dangerous when the cut was nearly made.

It took considerable skill and no little amount of the loggers' colorful lingo to handle timber of this size. Power saws came much later.

The northwest Oregon woods grew 'em big and fat. The Seaside Spruce Lumber Company worked this particular section. During World War I loggers of the northwest coast "mined" quantities of spruce, under military supervision, for fighter planes.

Courtesy Oregon Historical Society

Above: Visitor stares in disbelief at tremendous size of this burl, exhibited on grounds of Tillamook Historical Museum. They don't grow them like this anymore.

Courtesy Oney's, at Elsie

Left: Backcountry railroads weren't halted by the rugged up-and-down country of the Coast Range, but created a network through the timberland. Many of the trestles were magnificent engineering feats, like this one being erected by a logging crew.

Above: Only geared Shay and Willamette lokeys could negotiate the ridgetops of the Tillamook Burn Country. Slow of pace, these plodding steamers were nevertheless able to move heavy log trains up steep grades. Timber companies invested fortunes in equipment like this.

Courtesy Oney's, at Elsie

Right: A Crown-Willamette working engine and crew pause at the Lewis & Clark Camp, probably after taking on water. Note coat, hat, and cable draped unceremoniously across the front of the lokey.

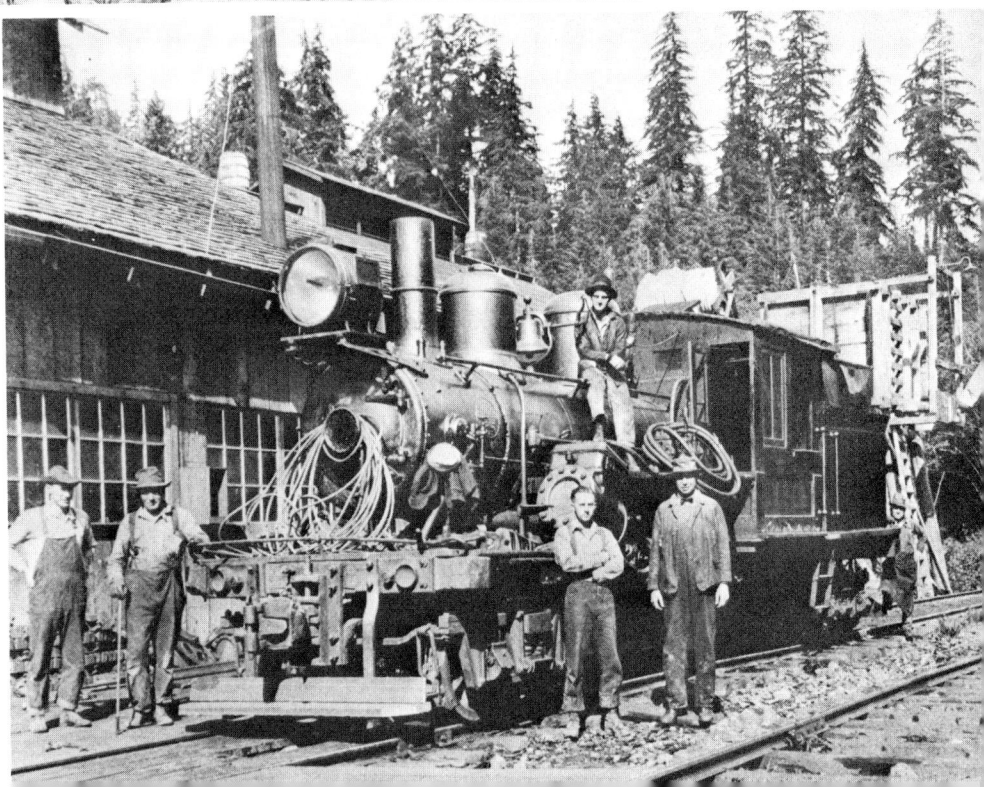

The Never-Still roundhouse lived up to its name. This was where logging locomotives and other rolling stock were kept in working order around the clock. It serviced equipment of the northern camps, among them Western Cooperage. Today, only railroad ghosts haunt the place.

Courtesy Oney's, at Elsie

Log dumps along the coast were many and busy. Logs were rafted up and headed for the sawmills. This six-spot Shay is making ready to splash its load at the Young's River dump, while at the Lewis & Clark dump, what was always a spectacular sight is in progress.

Courtesy Oney's, at Elsie

It took a lot of men to keep a big logging operation moving at highball. Somehow a photographer got this crew together for a picture at Tideport, four miles east of Elsie.

Courtesy Oney's, at Elsie

Logging camp life was often dull when off the job, and loggers proved to be irrepressible hams for photographers. This gang, demonstrating the unbelievable size of this tree, posed on terraced springboards.

Photo by Darius Kinsey   *Courtesy Mrs. A. C. Johannesen*

Like mining centers of the Old West, logging camps sprang up throughout the heavily timbered Tillamook country. Largest was near Glenwood, later called the Consolidated Camp. The camp was laid out in 1921 by A. C. Johannesen for the Big Creek Logging Company about two miles above Glenwood. Most of the buildings are now gone, but two remain as repair shops for an historical trolley park collection.

Courtesy Oney's, at Elsie

Logging centers were scattered throughout the region. Often they were tied to logging railroads, a sure method for loggers and officials to travel to town. Other camps were more isolated. "Tideport," owned by Brix-Woodward near Elsie, had its railroad. Camp McGregor was another huge center, with bunks for two hundred loggers.

Courtesy Oney's, at Elsie

What was called the "Single Man's Logging Camp" was typical of many in the tall timber. This camp was located on Young's River. Mostly they were the same, with loggers' shacks seen against hill at left and cookshack and dining hall built beside the railroad. Some buildings were on trucks to be moved from place to place.

33

More and more the big timber of northwest Oregon was being felled, bucked, and shipped to the many mills spread from the coast along the Columbia and Willamette rivers, hauled on the long pole trains of the P.R.&N. and the Columbia rail route.

Fire patrol methods were as primitive and weak as the few laws, and often after the fact. Timber companies had their own private Northwest Forest Protective Association, which dealt with fires after they'd started, rather than preventing them. Since the woods were filled with outdoors people, fires might come from most any source, not merely logging, which was most often blamed. Wardens and spotters patrolled the woods in summers from crude lookouts in the Trask and Cedar Butte areas. Leonard Rush is shown on ladder waving to a 1918 photographer.

Life of the wardens was often isolated, with little outside contact, as at Trask headquarters. Runners were used to report fires. Trails and roads were sparse. Lightning fires might start deep in the backcountry, requiring crews to hike many hours to reach a blaze.

The Trask lookout had a rural telephone with crank and even a "booth" resembling an outhouse. Names of the warden and his dog have been lost in time.

A. A. Sergersten was the 1918 warden at Cedar Butte. Howard Reeher and Tom Stevenson also served as lookouts at Cedar Butte.

Courtesy Oney's, at Elsie

"Watch your fires" says the 1923 warning sign on the left, at the beginning of the trail up Saddle Mountain. The letters "C.W.P." probably indicate this was a Crown-Willamette protection area. Headquarters for the entire region were at Forest Grove, with Cecil Kyle the chief warden. There were subdistricts at Jewell, near Seaside, and Tillamook. Although a state forester existed, he had little power. These were primarily private lands, and protection was in the hands of the companies that owned them.

Thus, the huge timberland held sway over most everything, and life's patterns were shaped according to its moods. Yet in the summer of 1933 this breathtaking wilderness was suffering under a long, extremely hot, and dry time, unlike anything experienced within memory on the northwest coast. The woods were explosive, and by August there was mounting fear for the forest itself, as if it were poised on the brink of disaster.

Chapter Two

THE GREAT DISASTER

"We never denied that we had a fire that day. But ours wasn't the only one. There was another one that started maybe four or five hours before our fire had started."

William H. Lyda

THE NORTHWEST WOODS had never been drier than in that midsummer of 1933. Even the coastal forests of Oregon and Washington were parched tinder dry, without the usual damp cooling fogs which, on the hottest days, drift silently inland to bring relief to both timber and wildlife.

Rivers ran low, streams dried up, animals and birds suffered and died from the heat and lack of moisture. The danger from fire — and very likely a big one — was on all sides, a constant worry among the thousands of people in the towns that fringed this great, old-growth wilderness and those living in the backcountry. A carelessly tossed cigarette, an abandoned campfire, a sudden lightning storm, a reckless logger — any small spark might ignite these woods into a conflagration that nothing could stop.

In early August humidity plunged to record lows. The threat of fire hung in the very air of this Great Depression year, when safety regulations and laws were very general and without teeth. Ignorance over the relationship of humidity to fire dangers was widespread; use of hygrometers and psychrometers was scattered and had limited acceptance. Few logging operators possessed them. Wardens and patrols were small in number, and communications were such that runners were used to inform logging operators when a shutdown became necessary. Thus, the stage was set for one of the greatest and most devastating forest fires of all time, that would even dwarf the destructive eruption of Mount St. Helens nearly half a century later. As with St. Helens, when the Tillamook forest blew up, it reshaped life of the region and much of Oregon for all future time.

Nobody has ever documented, at least to my knowledge, the ways in which the great fire caused life and times to switch directions. We weren't as socially alert as we are today, nor as concerned over the environment. The tragedy of total destruction of a fine wilderness — a national treasure — was shrugged off as would any other kind of natural disaster, as "just something that happened."

It was regretted, for sure, but nothing could be done about it. Trees were cheap and often times useless plants. As for the wildlife, the game and birds would come back. Oregon and the Pacific Northwest had such an abundance of both that only faint concern was expressed over the losses, largely by minorities such as unhappy anglers and hunters. If the joys of hiking and camping in these great woods were wiped away, at least for a few years, outdoor types would have to seek another forest. Only later would the full realization hit home, that this land wouldn't come back easily, and things would never be quite the same.

The great fire changed many things, most notably a heavy impact upon the Oregon and Pacific Northwest economy. Logging and lumbering were the region's Number One industry, so that the killing of all those great trees was a multi-million dollar loss in a merchantable product and thousands of jobs in years to come. Unhappily, that same holocaust also created jobs in fighting the fires and later in the tremendous salvage effort of the 1930s and 1940s. In many respects, the impact of that fateful time is still being felt today.

As we shall see more than the obvious went up in the flames of that tremendous conflagration. Those tiny first sparks held all the power of a splitting atom, and nobody will ever know for certain how or why it happened, only that it did. The logging operator claimed it was sabotage; that three flashlight lenses were found where the Gales Creek fire broke out, suspected to have been placed there by an outbid competitor for the job. Under the conditions of those woods that August, it was entirely possible. So would have been two branches rubbing together from a passing deer or elk, a spark from a locomotive or machinery, or metal rubbing on metal. The origin of the second fire to the south or southwest has never been disclosed, except that Bill Lyda, who was at his father's logging operation on upper Gales Creek that day, said he learned "that there was a big whingding party in there the day before; and next morning a woman called down to Forest Grove, asking someone to come get her and the kids as they were surrounded by fire."

Testimony was substantial by those claiming to have seen another fire burning *ahead* of the one in Gales Creek Canyon. It all revolves round whether sparks from Gales Creek, carried on upper air currents, ignited the other fire, or whether Fire No. 2 was indeed "out in front." Secret or unpublicized post-fire hearings (timber outfits, like gold camp miners, appear to have had their own law) fixed the blame on the Gales Creek Logging Company, despite testimony to the contrary. The question will never be fully settled. But a big fire would likely have happened anyway, all things considered, for these woods and the thousands who lived in their shadows had an appointment with destiny . . .

Courtesy Oney's, at Elsie

Public forestry was notably weak, both in manpower and effective laws. Forest protective associations were under the control and jurisdiction of timber companies, which were interested primarily in protecting their own timberlands and those of adjacent neighbors. Yet, the Oregon State Board of Forestry distributed this classic poster voicing concern over carelessness with fire. With a four-letter word in large type, it is far removed from the Keep Green posters and bumper stickers of the present.

This "fire warden," Bob Feggers, used his horse, Pinto, to get around the backcountry, to check logging operators, anglers, and hunters, and to extinguish abandoned campfires. But his authority was limited; many people held little respect for these early wardens or for the few laws that backed them up.

Symbolic of early-day forest protection were the flimsy lookouts scattered throughout big timber country.

Steam donkey rigs were common throughout Tillamook country. While loggers weren't anxious to burn up their livelihood, they were often careless with fire. Their operations were a constant risk in dry weather. An independent lot, some shut down when logging conditions were bad. Others ran "hoot owl" shifts at night or in the early morning, when the humidity would likely be higher. A third group took many risks, not the least being from their own men. Much of the equipment was also unsafe.

Courtesy Oney's, at Elsie

Gales Creek Logging Company setup along upper Gales Creek was similar to this one on that fateful day of August 14, 1933. There were more trees, however. Elmer Lyda, his son Bill, and their crew were logging across Gales Creek Canyon to a railroad loading dock for shipment to a sawmill at nearby Glenwood Camp. Fire broke out following lunch, before word came to shut down. Controversy existed as to whether the outfit hauled "one more log" after being told to close down, but this is now discounted as a myth and "loose talk" of the times. Elmer Lyda's logging company was blamed for many years for singly starting the Tillamook fire, allegedly through carelessness and perhaps irresponsibility. But at least one other fire was seen burning to the west, well beyond the summit. Its origin remains a mystery.

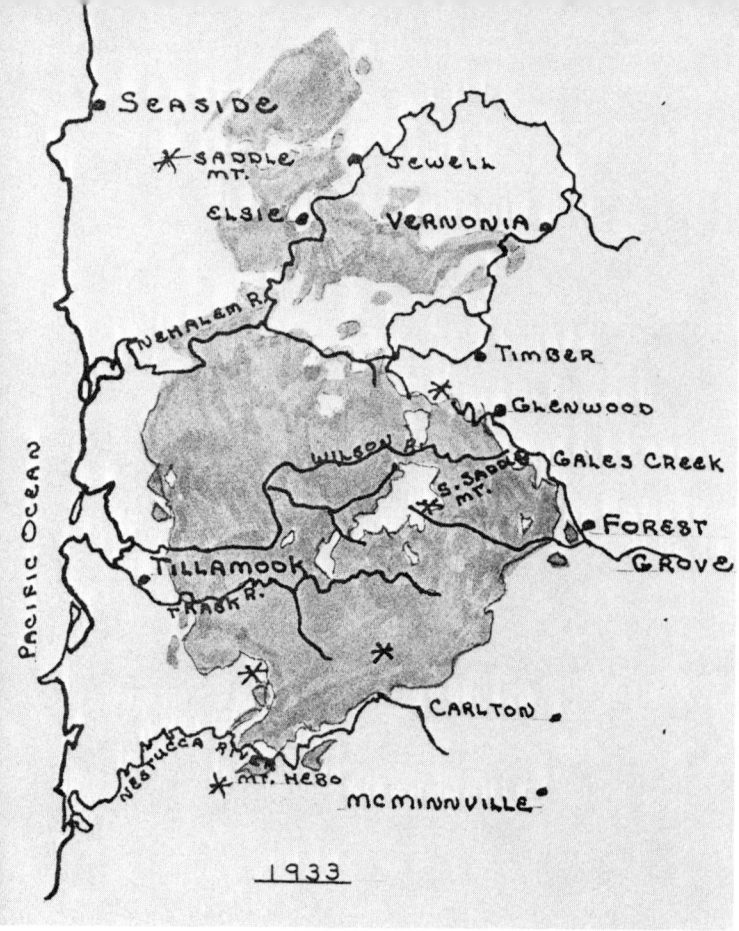

Left: Once started, nothing could stop the two or more fires that went on the rampage through the Tillamook forest. Nature took over, combining the worst possible conditions of low humidity, dry tinderbox woods, and no relief from fog or rain. Nine days later, the fires, which were by now one giant holocaust, literally blew up, ravaging 240,000 acres containing nearly twelve billion board feet of prime timber, mostly destroyed in twenty frightening hours.

Cecil Kyle was district warden for the privately financed Northwest Protective Association at the time of the Tillamook disaster.

Walter Vandervelden, chief of the crack volunteer fire department at Forest Grove, was an early arrival at the scene of the outbreak, bringing firefighting equipment. He later testified he saw a second fire.

Alf C. Johannesen was in charge of the logging operations for Crossett-Western. He arrived by railroad speeder from Glenwood thirty minutes too late to shut down the Lyda operation. By then the fire was well under way.

Lynn S. Cronemiller was state forester when the disaster struck. State foresters had little authority over logging operators at the time.

Local logging crews and volunteers were unable to stop the Gales Creek fire or reach the other one to the west. By the following day, the Gales Canyon fire was spreading over the first ridge.

The mounting fire, beginning to crown, galloped in all directions. What was originally two fires joined to become one. Later, someone purposefully set another to the north, adding to the growing holocaust. Before being finally controlled, the Tillamook disaster covered over a quarter million acres of rich timberland.

Courtesy Oregon Historical Society

In the first few days, the fire continued to grow. Spot fires were spreading over an eighteen-square-mile area. Fire fighters were pouring into the region, among them one thousand Civilian Conservation Corps (CCC) boys, crews from Mount Hood National Forest, and National Guard companies. For a brief time fog and cooler temperatures brought hope, but it was short-lived.

The fire was crowning everywhere, with flames leaping through the tall tree tops and building on their own updrafts. The hot, dry weather returned; in the ten days since the outbreaks, crews had met with little success corraling the conflagration.

On the memorable day of August 24 the fire literally exploded, becoming a rampaging giant that nothing could stop, traveling at high speed, and destroying all in its path. The holocaust was likened to an atomic bomb of a decade later, its mushroom cloud boiling more than forty thousand feet into the atmosphere, visible for hundreds of miles at sea and inland. During an incredible twenty hours, the fire rampaged across 220,000 acres, burning trees at the rate of 600,000 board feet an hour.

Above: Along a fifteen-mile front the fire created an awesome orange wall of flame, while hurricane winds built by the flames' updraft toppled and uprooted giant firs, hurtling them great distances. One CCC fire fighter, Frank Palmer from Illinois, was killed by a falling tree near the Shorb camp.

Left: When the fire blew up, thousands were forced to flee. Mary Watters was working near Cochran as a logging camp waitress at Camp 4, Wheeler Logging Company, when orders came to evacuate. She buried her trunk of personal possessions. A train of empty log cars backed into the camp to take out some two hundred refugees. Then the fire turned another direction, and evacuation was unnecessary.

Photos courtesy Jean Ackerson Spiering

A group of Portland Camp Fire Girls, on a trail ride to the coast, was nearly trapped by the blowup and had to flee for their lives. The young riders left the Crackerbox Ranch on the southern fringe of the Tillamook forest, heading for Davis and Blaine via Hell's Canyon and Devil's Playground. Making seventeen miles the first day, they trailed through the bleached snags of an old burn before setting up camp. A ranger came in, warning them to get out. The girls and escorts made a night ride, crossing the Nestucca River eight times before reaching the safety of the coast. In places they could see the fast-traveling fire and feel the heat. They never forgot the adventure. Shown in camp scene, from left: Bill Oberteuffer, Gilbert Lee, Ann Hutchinson, Sally Hunt, Martha Howes, Frank Larwood, Nancy Hunt, Ruth Howes, Jean Ackerson, Alice Ann Thomas, and Charles Clanaghan. Third view shows group fleeing the fire.

Photo by Oliver Matthews

Above: "The fire has been feeding largely on beauty," wrote Mary L. Roberts, a Forest Grove reporter. Northern Oregon beaches were buried two feet deep in ash and debris, which also fell on ships five hundred miles at sea and on Boise, Idaho. The great smoke cloud was seen in Montana. This view was taken in the Seine and Lee Creek area.

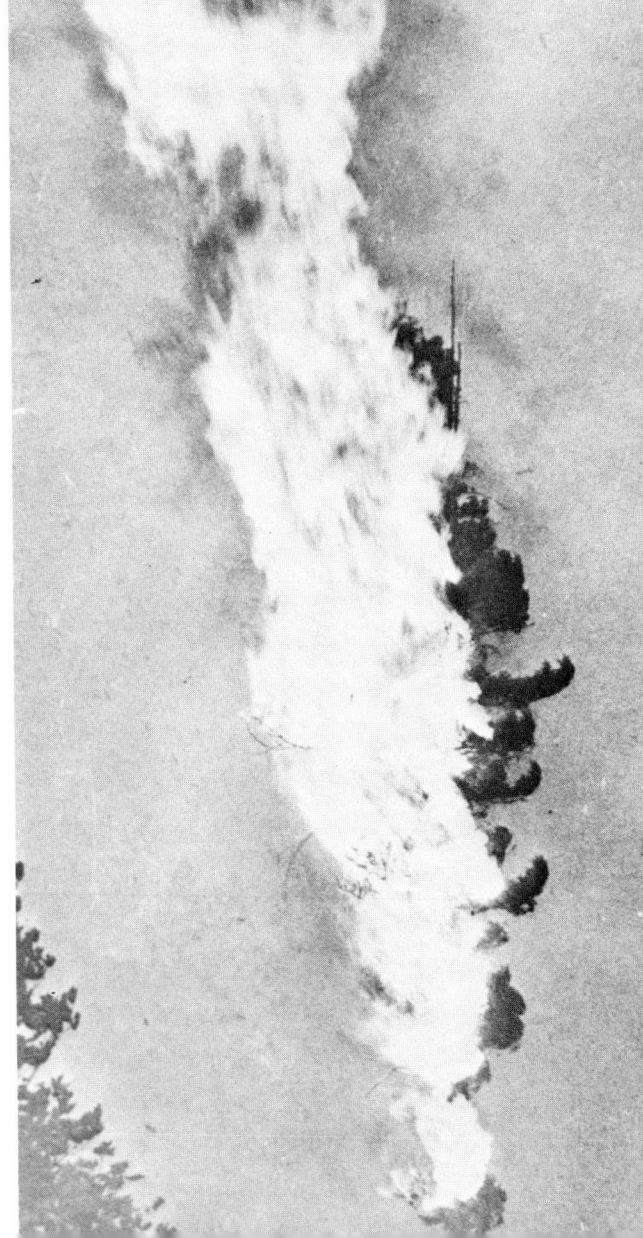

Photo by Les Ordman   Courtesy Oregon Historical Society

Right: Trying to control such a crown fire was next to impossible. The fire went on the rampage, in full flame in seconds. The updraft wind is blowing the nearby tree at left.

Courtesy Oregon Historical Society

Three thousand fire fighters were dispatched to the northwestern Oregon area. Many were volunteers, for this was Great Depression time and a chance for some pay.

Newly arrived fire fighters pick up digging tools. Many of these men were young greenhorns, especially the CCC boys from back East, who had never before seen a forest fire. Crews were generally helpless when flames leaped the trails. Some became trapped by fast-moving flames, but the death toll was kept amazingly low.

Courtesy Oregon Historical Society

Fire camps and outposts were quickly set up at accessible locations. Sometimes outposts were forced to evacuate. The location of this chow line is unknown, but from the camp's haphazard appearance, it was spur-of-the-moment.

Day after day, and into the hot humid nights, the fire continued to boil and blow, reaping additional havoc on life and natural wonders.

Photo by Everly Aircraft

Photo by Joe Bell

The heavy smoke from this unimaginable holocaust blotted out the sun, turning midday to night in coastal and valley towns. Joe Bell, a professional photographer, took this view of downtown Tillamook in midafternoon. The scene was repeated in other communities. Declared the *Tillamook Herald:* "A darkness grew in intensity as the day progressed. Lights were burned in homes and business houses all day. Farmers went to pastures for their cows at four o'clock. Small wonder that chickens had to be lifted from their roosts in the morning and roosters were crowing all day. . . . At Rockaway, white ashes fell steadily like a drifting snow storm."

The conflagration roared within eye and earshot of Tillamook, a frightening sight as recorded by W. D. Hagenstein, veteran forester with the West Coast Lumbermen's Association and the Industrial Forestry Association.

Photo by W. D. Hagenstein

Photo by Burton B. Thurber *Courtesy Oregon Historical Society*

Another fire raged to the north of the original outbreaks, south of Vernonia and in the Forest Grove region. This one was blamed on an arsonist, perhaps aiming at creating jobs during the Depression. Photographer Thurber made this view August 25, 1933, from eleven thousand feet from a Rasmussen-Meadows, Inc., plane piloted by James Lester Meadows. Jess Sills, pioneer movie news photographer, also recorded the big blowup. His film rests in files of the Oregon Historical Society.

The fire ate rapidly through prime green timber, into deep canyons, and across high ridges. Sometimes it skipped small tree clumps, as seen in mid-foreground. These might have eventually helped the forest to come back, but subsequent fires destroyed them, too.

Courtesy Oregon Historical Society

Frightening fireworks scenes were on all sides, consuming anything that lived. Even the soil was burned, while the wildlife loss was tremendous.

Above: The historic Trask House, that fine wilderness resort and stage stop, was leveled. Some of the hottest spots were in the Trask River country, where the fire burned with such fury that those areas couldn't be replanted fifty years later.

Courtesy Jerry D. Alto and Oregon Historical Society
Photo by Les Ordman

Left: Extremely hot weather fueled the flames to greater violence. Something of its fury is seen in this view of one mad canyon. That's a very hot fire in upper left corner of the picture.

Photo by Les Ordman *Courtesy Oregon Historical Society*

Fire raged down the steep canyons and cut the main-line railroad *(left)*, also destroying tunnels. Later, when the railroad was repaired, some tunnels were bypassed.

The flames roared over several counties. The tremendous size in both area and timber consumed is seen in this dramatic view of the huge smoke cloud. This section of the Coast Range is so rugged that many areas were inaccessible, making even token fire fighting and trailing virtually impossible.

Photo by Clarence T. Stanley

57

Courtesy Oregon Historical Society

Towns such as Elsie, Cochran, and Timber were constantly under siege. At times rumors said they had been completely destoyed. This bridge on the Devil's Lake Fork of the Wilson River was found smouldering by brave fire fighters who checked out the crossing.

Only black timbers remain of this crossing, with its broken roadway and the charred sticks strewn along the stream bed. Two college students, James Bushong of Forest Grove and Herbert Redtzke of Portland, were trapped at such a place and spent hours in a creekbed with deer and other wildlife to escape the raging flames.

Courtesy Larry Kemp

The loss in wildlife could never be imagined. Reporter Mary L. Roberts wrote: "The toll in wildlife must be immense. The dense forests provided shelter and sustenance for deer, rabbits, chipmunks, pine squirrels, gray squirrels, grouse, partridge and rodents, in addition to many bear and cougar. Some may have escaped, but inevitably the majority must have been trapped and burned. Without doubt, small birds by the thousands perished."

Courtesy Larry Kemp

Right: Communications were virtually wiped out, so fire fighters in various areas found it impossible to contact others to coordinate their efforts. Here, a lone lineman searches for the long-distance wire in the Trask Mountains. Radio was in its infancy, and shortwave contact was almost nonexistent.

Courtesy OSFD

Below: At long last, in September, the air began cooling and ocean fogs crept over the stricken region. The punch went out of the holocaust, leaving only smouldering ruins such as this grim scene near a Wilson River Highway bridge.

Courtesy John Coats

Great quantities of logging equipment scattered over the region were destroyed. Many loggers, especially the gypos, could ill-afford the losses. They were already hard hit by the Great Depression.

To protect the sleds from being destroyed, donkey engines in the path of the Tillamook fire were banked with earth.

Courtesy John Coats

Courtesy John Coats

This was once a fairyland forest. Sorry scenes such as this were everywhere. Lumberman John Coats was among the few who used his camera during and after the holocaust. Unlike today, not everyone had a camera, even a Brownie, and few could afford the film.

When the fire finally died, Oregonians looked in horror and disbelief at the destruction. Much was unrecognizable; even familiar landmarks were completely gone. Private hearings in Portland, despite conflicting testimony, blamed the Lydas for the great fire.

Courtesy Oregon Historical Society

Courtesy U.S. Forest Service

In the aftermath, a new American desert was created, stretching in all directions to the far horizons. Natural seed sources were destroyed, giving scant hope that the trees might come back. Salvage operations began shortly after the conflagration to meet the threat of disease and renewed fires. This would continue for decades.

Courtesy U.S. Forest Service

Desolation . . . in every direction

Three years later the coastal town of Bandon, Oregon, was destroyed by another mighty fire which started from a logging operation and spread into combustable Irish gorse surrounding the town. These two frightening, destructive events, and successive large conflagrations throughout the thirties and early forties, brought about revolutionary changes demanded by both the public and visionaries within the timber industry. It was also realized that any attempted reforestation was impossible until fire could be controlled.

Chapter Three

AGAIN ... AND AGAIN ... AND AGAIN ...

"That Tillamook Burn is jinxed, I tell ya. It's gonna burn every six years!"

Logger to Author

BY THE TIME the Tillamook Burn exploded a third time, in the dry, hot summer of 1945, loggers were convinced that the tragic region was under a "six-year jinx." A major fire would happen every half-dozen years, and nothing could alter that fact. In the intervening years, lesser conflagrations would break out, adding more acres to the already scarred and blackened tinderbox.

One would think there was little left to burn. But flames found combustibles in the deadfalls, debris, vine maple, underbrush, young seedlings trying to grow, and also in the thousands of snags, bleached by summer suns, that marched across the many steep miles of the huge Burn.

The causes were numerous, encouraged by a succession of long, dry summers. One of the leading culprits was the public itself — careless smokers, and abandoned campers' and hunters' fires. During World War II Japanese incendiary balloons floated thousands of miles across the Pacific Ocean and ignited at least one fire in the Tillamook Burn. Lightning and logging caused other outbreaks. Laws requiring spark arrestors on machinery and steam locomotives were either ignored or nonexistent; it was wartime, and salvage logging was a war industry.

Because of the continual fires, nature never had a chance to make a comeback. Each fire reburned the wasteland and sacrificed new charred acres of standing old growth that had previously escaped the flames, as well as natural seedlings struggling upward through the fireweed. That the Tillamook would never come back, at least not for generations, seemed a strong possibility.

Loggers weren't the only ones to believe that it was impossible to keep fires from the Tillamook Burn. Many so-called "experts" reached the same conclusion. Only the loggers, with their characteristic practicality, put it in the simplest terms. They were a superstitious lot anyway, and had a right to be, for they lived with danger and sudden death.

"The simplest approach is to regard the entire Burn as being beyond justifiable human effort, to surround it with a superfireline and let nature take its course, whether it takes 100 or 300 years to grow a new forest," declared a U.S. Forest Service report of October 1945. "While such an approach is extremely pessimistic, it is much sounder than a continuance of protection expenditures at the present level."

The danger was, of course, that not only were the fires continuing, but the do-nothing years were slipping by, and erosion was filling Tillamook Bay, wiping the last vestiges of hope from the wasteland. The 1939 and 1945 fires were major disasters, combining many of the same elements that had caused the original conflagration. The 1939 fire blackened around 200,000 acres, with 834,220,000 board feet of timber killed. In 1945, the rampaging flames covered 180,130 acres and charred 439,985,000 board feet. Whatever was tried was too little and too late, whether it was protection from fires or the planting of trees.

Thus, on pressure from citizens and public officials, a series of meetings began, to last throughout the winter of 1945–46. The first was held at Forest Grove, in the shadow of the Big Burn, with about thirty key people turning out. State Senator Paul L. Patterson of Hillsboro, who would later become governor, chaired the lengthy session.

Judge Harland M. Wood of Tillamook County expressed the point of view of the loggers:

"We are going to have a fire in another few years because nothing has been done about it, and nothing is going to be done about it."

The loggers' attitude that the region was "jinxed" was dangerous. You could talk yourself into a fire, as you could talk yourself into an illness; and beyond that, there was also that lone itinerant woodsman who might set a fire, just to prove the point. . . .

The "six-year jinx" seemed to be just that. The fires of 1939, 1945, and 1951 added to the scarred forest lands, as shown by the shaded areas of these maps. In many ways the later holocausts seemed haunting repetitions of the original fire. The fire of 1939 added 50,091 new acres to the wasteland, while 1945 blackened 65,150 acres, killing an additional 1,274,205,000 board feet of timber.

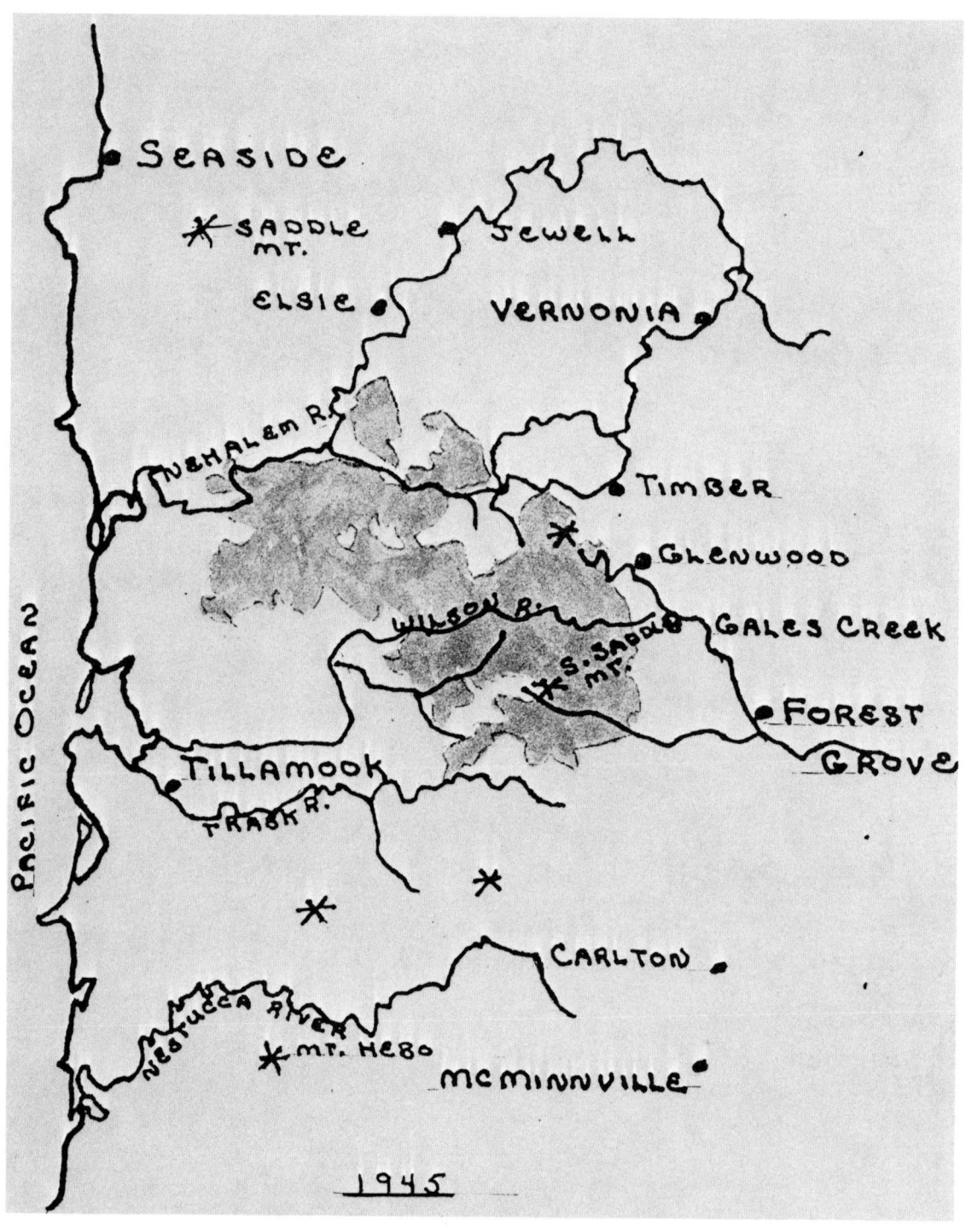

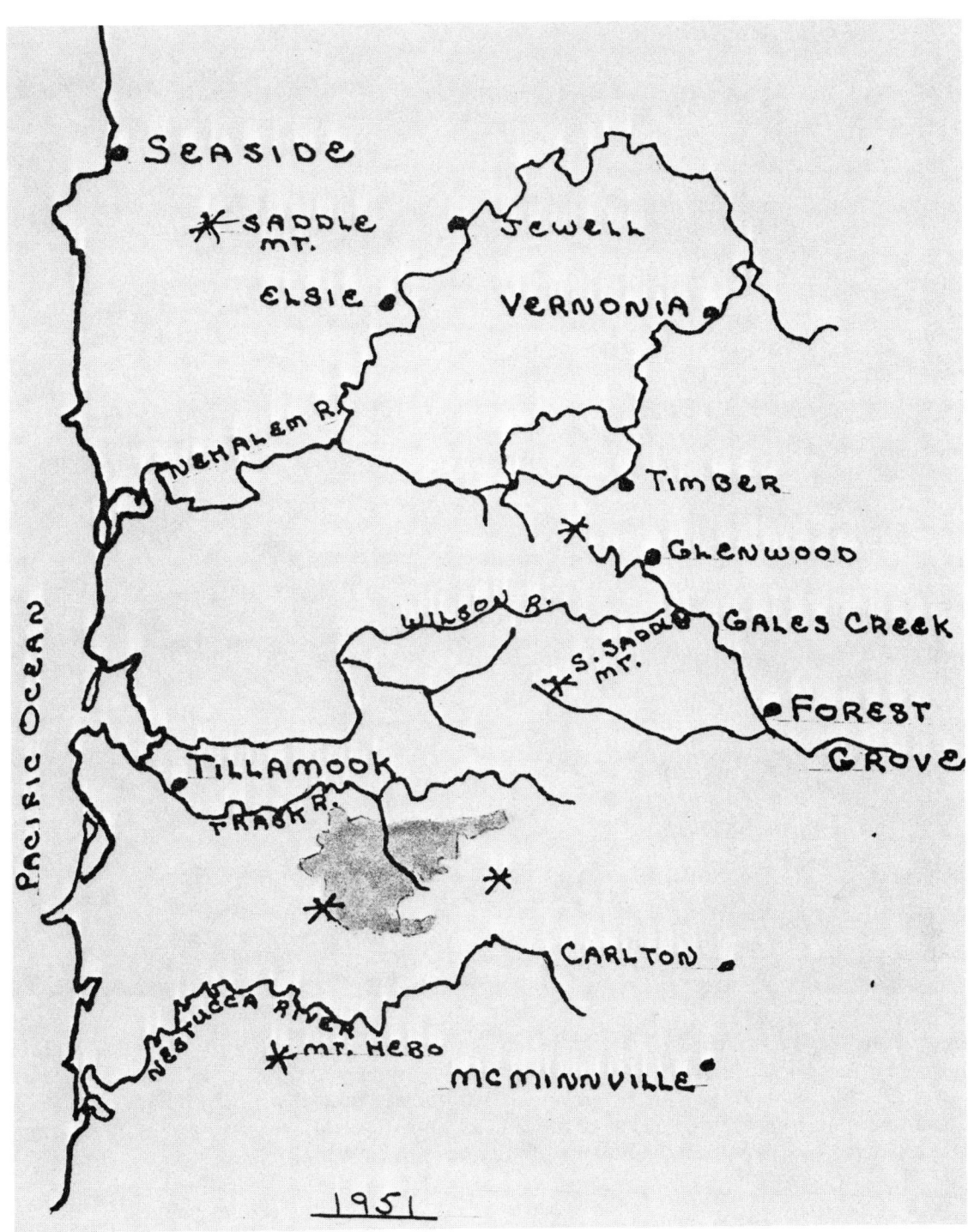

Photo by Ellis Lucia

A lone logger, Pete Walker, watches his world go up in smoke once again, shortly after the outbreak of the 1951 jinx-year fire, west of Cherry Grove in Elkhorn Canyon, near where the celebrated Trask House once stood. Three 1951 fires in that same area were much smaller. By then the rehabilitation program had been launched, incorporating a new fire-fighting blueprint. In four days the fire was trailed, but it spread over twenty thousand acres, mostly within the bounds of previous burns. With this fire, foresters turned the corner.

The atomic bomb was born a few years later, near the end of World War II, but residents of northwestern Oregon already had a clear idea how it would look. The 1939 holocaust mushroomed into the atmosphere much the same as in 1933. This was the view near Forest Grove from forestry headquarters, then still a private protective association.

Courtesy Oregon Historical Society

The 1939 fire was as vicious as that of 1933, traveling fast and fanned by high winds. It wiped out the huge Floras Logging Company operations, including the last of its green timber, in this spectacular nighttime inferno. Oregon-American timber operations were also hard hit, with fourteen million board feet of dressed logs destroyed, plus five railroad trestles, two locomotives, and fifteen steam donkeys.

Many logging operations were burned in this second big Tillamook fire. The flames moved in all directions, again threatening Tillamook and smaller communities. Ash, sparks, and debris fell on northern coastal beaches. Dwyer Logging lost five steam donkeys and five million board feet of cut logs. Trask-Willamette's camp was leveled, along with many others. Four thousand fire fighters couldn't get the flames under control. After four weeks, the rains came.

A valiant crew is trying to save this railroad trestle in the Saddle Mountain area, near Benson siding, in salvage slash during the 1939 conflagration. Backfiring has been ignited at the base of the trestle, as a locomotive pushes a water tank into play. Hose may be seen extending from tank car, at the lower left of center.

Photo by William G. Morris *Courtesy USFS*

Photo by William G. Morris   Courtesy USFS

Smoke and flames broke loose near the Wolf Creek Highway during the 1939 holocaust. Bill Morris took this view August 4 on what were Oregon-American lands. Many people referred to the 1939 inferno as the "Wolf Creek Fire."

Near Quartz Creek bridge, salvage logging slash was blackened, adding to the already huge devastation
Photo by William G. Morris   *Courtesy USFS*

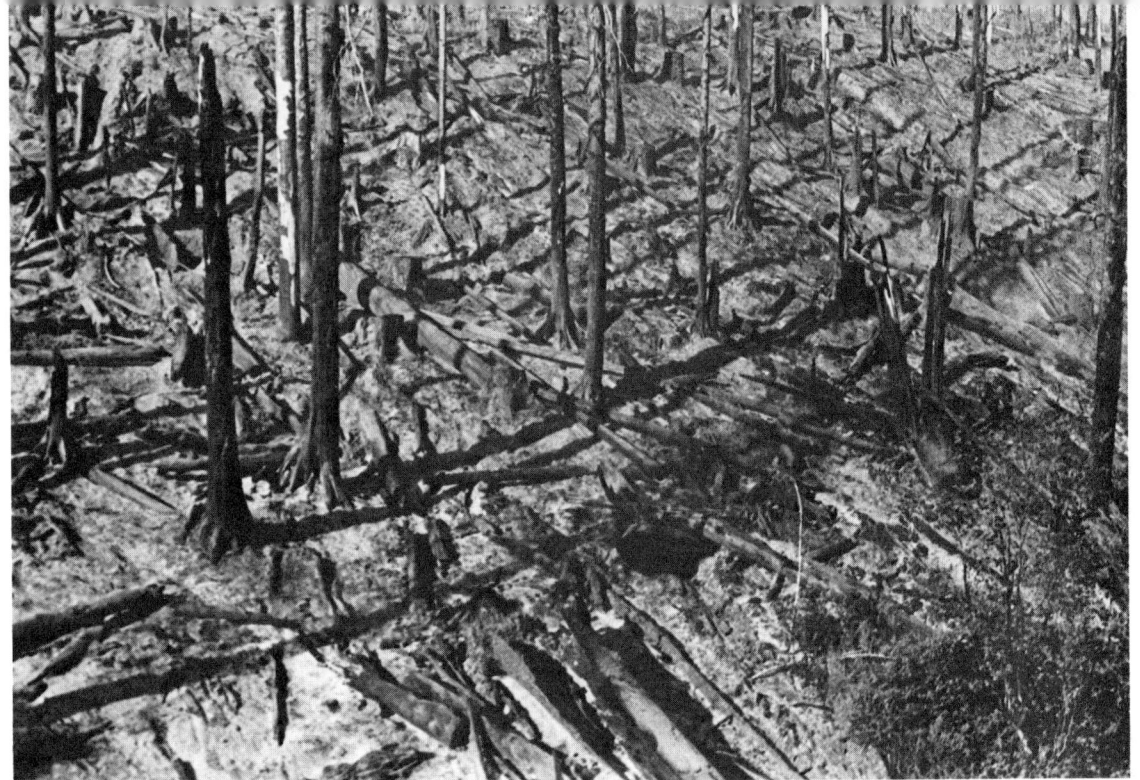

Photo by William G. Morris *Courtesy USFS*

Its beauty completely gone, this is how one section of The Burn looked following the 1939 fire.

Two years later, in 1941, the land showed little change, other than fireweed and some vine maple trying to gain a foothold. This view was west of Timber, near the Wolf Creek Highway.

Photo by George L. Griffith *Courtesy USFS*

Photo by Charles A. Rondt *Courtesy USFS*
The tragedy of the 1939 fire was that it burned into green timber, such as along this ridge, which might have seeded denuded slopes below to become a new forest. This wiped out any hope of natural reseeding.

Photo by Allan J. de Lay
One would think there was nothing left to burn, but somehow sparks were forever having their way, in snags, deadfalls, and young trees. Air pollution wasn't a concern then, at least publicly, but sights like this near public highways sickened Oregonians.

Courtesy Oregon Historical Society

Again in 1945 the Tillamook cut loose, just as World War II was ending. Aerial photos were restricted at the time by wartime censorship but later were released. This picture shows how fire was eating into stands of green timber.

Oregonians didn't have to wait the Fourth of July for spectacular fireworks. Sparks, firebrands, and flames ignited canyons and draws and traveled the ridges among the ghostlike snags. The 1945 conflagration added another 65,000 acres to the wasteland, bringing the total to 354,936 acres.

Photo by Les Ordman   *Courtesy Oregon Historical Society*

Courtesy Oregon Historical Society

Left: Fire fighters found it hard, dangerous work trailing around hot spots which flared up without warning.

Below: State Forester Nelson Rogers (*left*) conducted Oregon Gov. Earl Snell to the rim of the 1,700-foot Salmonberry Canyon to view the smouldering ruins of a once-fine forest. Neither lived to see the rehabilitation program begin, although it was Rogers' dream.

Courtesy Oregon Historical Society

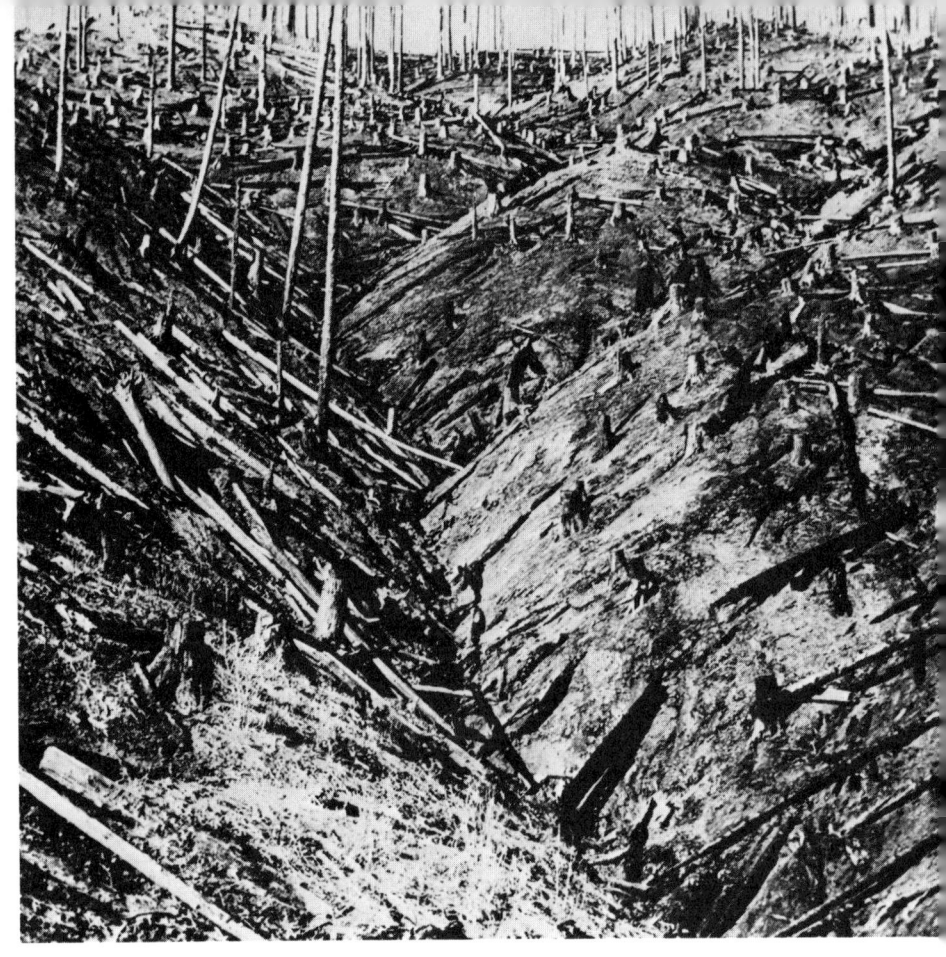

Right: More dead and blackened wasteland remained after the 1945 holocaust. For those who remembered the old forest and its beauty, sights like this brought sadness and anger.

Courtesy Oregon Historical Society

Below: The third great fire grabbed headlines from World War II, as both press and public became more vocal in their concern over the drab wasteland. Manpower was still short, so high school boys manned the firelines. Today, girls would also join the battle. The Ralph Gambles (*upper left*) lost their home, along with other families.

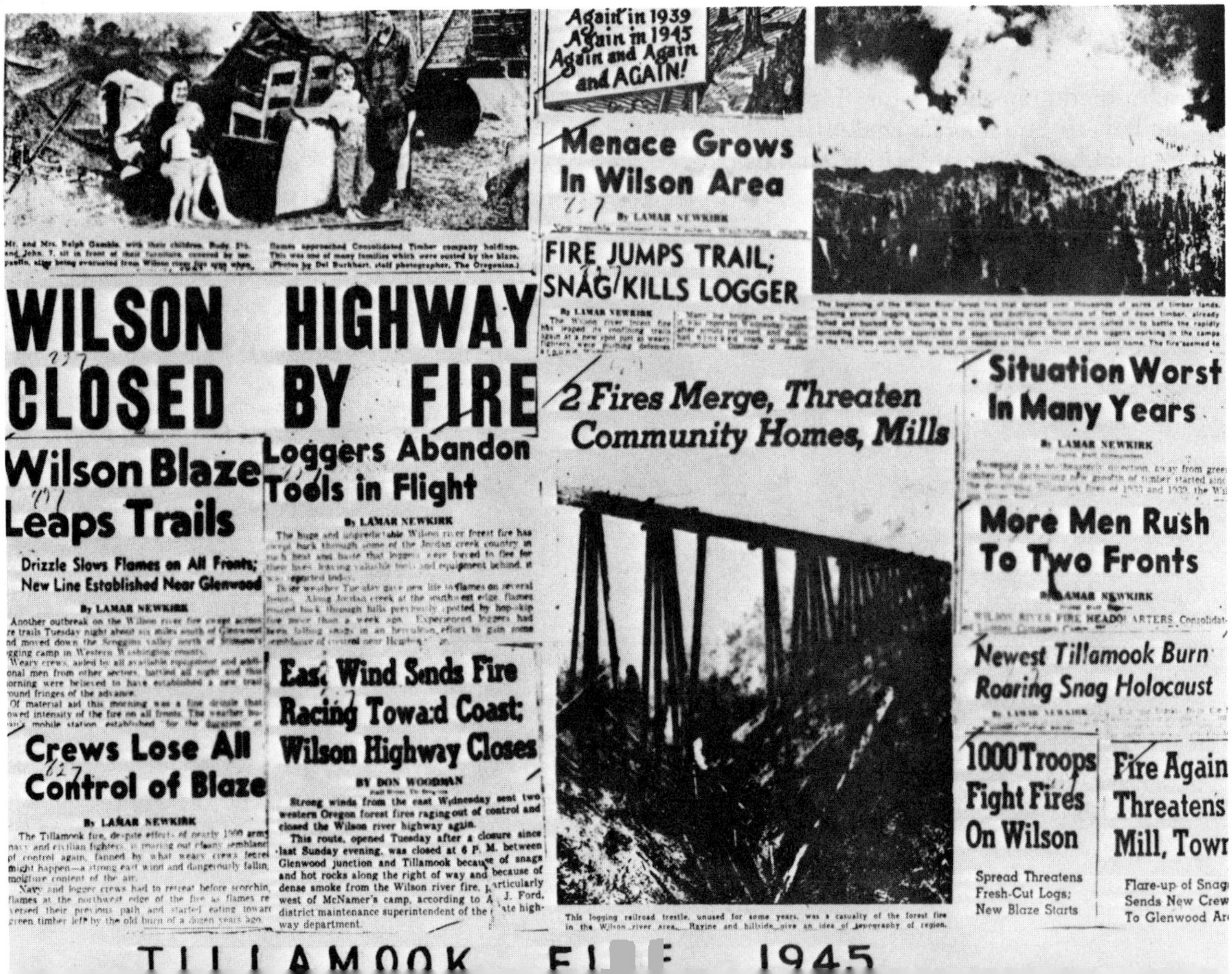

Again in 1939
Again in 1945
Again and Again
and AGAIN!

Menace Grows In Wilson Area

By LAMAR NEWKIRK

FIRE JUMPS TRAIL; SNAG KILLS LOGGER

By LAMAR NEWKIRK

WILSON HIGHWAY CLOSED BY FIRE

Situation Worst In Many Years

By LAMAR NEWKIRK

2 Fires Merge, Threaten Community Homes, Mills

Wilson Blaze Leaps Trails

Drizzle Slows Flames on All Fronts; New Line Established Near Glenwood

By LAMAR NEWKIRK

Loggers Abandon Tools in Flight

By LAMAR NEWKIRK

More Men Rush To Two Fronts

Newest Tillamook Burn Roaring Snag Holocaust

East Wind Sends Fire Racing Toward Coast; Wilson Highway Closes

BY DON WOODMAN

Strong winds from the east Wednesday sent two western Oregon forest fires raging out of control and closed the Wilson river highway again.

This route, opened Tuesday after a closure since last Sunday evening, was closed at 6 P. M. between Glenwood junction and Tillamook because of snags and hot rocks along the right of way and because of dense smoke from the Wilson river fire, particularly west of McNamer's camp, according to A. J. Ford, district maintenance superintendent of the state highway department.

Crews Lose All Control of Blaze

By LAMAR NEWKIRK

1000 Troops Fight Fires On Wilson

Spread Threatens Fresh-Cut Logs; New Blaze Starts

Fire Again Threatens Mill, Town

Flare-up of Snags Sends New Crew To Glenwood Area

This logging railroad trestle, unused for some years, was a casualty of the forest fire in the Wilson river area. Ravine and hillside give an idea of topography of region.

TILLAMOOK [illegible] 1945

Almost like clockwork, the Tillamook Burn ignited again in 1951 on the upper Trask River, west of Cherry Grove. The sight from the Tillamook dairyland country was a playback of other years.

The 1951 fire burned dramatically, but this time fire fighters hit it extra hard and were better organized. It blackened more than thirty-two thousand acres, mostly within bounds of past infernos.

Basil Hall manned a pumper hose to help control the 1951 fire before it could run completely amuck.

Courtesy Oregon Historical Society

Photo by Hans Running *Courtesy Oregon Historical Society*

A ridgetop at Camp Murphy provided a grandstand view of the new fire in Elkhorn Canyon after it broke out on July 20, 1951. Loggers blasting a tree top for a new spar, in near 100-degree weather, set off the blaze.

A district forester explains the path of the fire to newspaper reporter Leverett Richards. Foresters feared that if the blaze broke loose, the new rehabilitation program would suffer a severe setback with the public which had voted the financing.

Photo by Allan J. de Lay

Foresters quickly set up fire camps, anticipating a long siege if the blaze again ran rampant. The man, left of center, appears to be preparing to feed hungry fire fighters.

Fire camp at Murphy saw action on the 1951 North Fork blaze. Curtis Nesheim (*right*), in charge of fighting the fire as protection assistant forester, confers with Eino Winters. Adolph Berglund is in background.

The North Fork fire continued to grow as fighters endeavored to trail around it. Much of the fire was in snags and deadfalls, and some salvaged logs. In many sections, there was little left of value.

Fire lines of the North Fork outbreak are easily defined in this aerial. Dark line in lower center shows how fire has been trailed with bulldozers. Fire has evidently jumped lines (*upper center*) into other stands of snags. A convoy of motorized equipment is barely visible along the road in the center.

At last, the fire appeared to be dying amid the rubble.

Much logging equipment was destroyed by the 1951 fire, along with salvage logs, seen strewn beyond the rig. The fire again wiped out Ginsberg Point, climbed Gold Peak, and moved south to Grindstone Mountain. It burned almost to the village of Trask and climbed Edwards Butte.

Steam donkeys and quantities of logging gear were lo in the flames; others were rendered useless. By today logging standards, these machines would appear o small value. But for the time and place, the loss wa equally as great to logging companies and gypos.

Once again the flames died away, and nature tried to patch up the disaster with fireweed, fern, and vine maple. Foresters realized that any kind of reforestation was impossible until fires could be eliminated from this rugged wasteland.

Courtesy American Forest Institute

Chapter Four

THE TILLAMOOK COAL MINERS

Within three months after The Fire, while the loggers could still warm their hands and feet at smoking windfalls, long trains loaded with coal-black logs were rolling down off the hills.

Stewart H. Holbrook

ASHES AND TIMBERS of the great Tillamook Fire of 1933 were hardly cold and many still smouldering when loggers returned to this sorry land in what became one of the most amazing salvage efforts of all time.

Salvaging The Burn, which sprawled across several counties in rugged, extremely mountainous terrain, boggled the mind. Estimates were that 12.5 billion board feet of timber had been killed during the August holocaust. Sawed into boards, it would supply all the lumber demands for all the sawmills of the United States during a single year. Stacked beside the Empire State Building, then the world's tallest man-made structure, it would put the skyscraper in shadow. Closer home, it would dwarf the Cascade peaks.

It proved to be one of the strangest of all logging operations. The loggers worked in thick ash, standing on springboards amid charred remains of the deadfalls, felling huge coal black giants with misery whips, as they had always done. There were no power saws. When the trees dropped, huge choking clouds of ash exploded skyward, making breathing difficult. It was miserable work; the loggers became so dirty from soot and ash that they appeared blackface, at times unable to recognize each other. They called themselves the "Tillamook Minstrels" and the "Tillamook Coal Miners."

Timber owners quickly organized, for time was of the essence. Even in those embryo years of forestry, practical loggers and lumbermen realized that much of the fire-ravaged timber remained sound, that worms, bugs, and disease would be the far greater threats of destruction. They met with public officials and key civic leaders in what evolved into an astounding spirit of cooperation. The stricken lumber-logging outfits combined their resources into the Consolidated Timber Company, a bold cooperative enterprise, with Lloyd R. Crosby in charge. He was of long seasoning in the woods, highly competent, and imaginative. The speed and efficiency with which Consolidated got out the black timber became legendary, especially during World War II. The military was so impressed that Consolidated was awarded the coveted Army-Navy E for its wartime production effort.

Probably it was never considered at the time, but the great salvage effort also became the initial step in bringing back the land to full productivity. As a first step, The Burn had to be cleaned up to lessen the fire dangers. And while the logging contributed to the fire hazard, it also reduced the rubble and the numbers of snags during the next ten-to-fifteen years, without any cost to taxpayers. Had the initial salvage never happened, the task eventually might have been all too overwhelming and costly to bring back the land at all. The blade cut two ways: logging operations caused fires which destroyed tiny new trees seeded naturally and trying to survive, but these same operations helped prepare the land for eventual reforestation.

American Forest Products Industries
Photo by Arthur W. Priaulx   Courtesy Forest History Society
Above, left: Loggers trying to salvage blackened timber were called "coal miners." It proved to be dirty, wretched work, one of the world's oddest logging operations. Loggers covered with soot and ash emerged unable to recognize each other.

Courtesy Forest History Society
Above, right: Despite their appearance, the black trees were sound within. Only their bark was charred by fires. The ominous threat was from beetles, worms, and disease.

Photo by Hugh Ackroyd
Left: The traditional tools of the loggers — the ax and the crosscut saw — were still used in felling and bucking salvage timber in the Tillamook Burn. Thus, the pace with which the job was done was considered astonishing. Power saws were nonexistent and would enter The Burn only in later years, during World War II and the postwar era.

Courtesy Washington County Historical Museum

Loggers worked along steep slopes, with rubble and deadfalls strewn over the ground. Logger Floyd Racine, in cloth hat, is straddling a black deadfall. Arnold Raymond balances on springboard while he works with crosscut to drop this huge timber in the Trask area, hard hit by the fire.

It was a dead forest in the early years, with little foliage and scant wildlife. This skidder is working at salvage logging against a background of snags and deadfalls. In contrast to the Mount St. Helens salvaging fifty years later, machinery and logging equipment were primitive, but this was all that was available at the time.

Courtesy OSFD

Courtesy Jerry D. Alto

Left: As salvage work progressed, the sorry land was dotted with charred stumps, another permanent symbol of the Tillamook Burn, as were the black snags which later were bleached gray by the sun.

While many logging and lumbering methods were changing, muscle power remained the lone way of dropping the trees. Demonstrating salvage logging is Curtis Nesheim (*right*) who later became chief fire warden of the northwest Oregon district. On the other end of this misery whip is Ellis ("Blackie") Blackmore.

Courtesy Curtis Nesheim

Salvage logging seemed often like a giant game of jackstraws or pick-up-sticks, as shown in this 1937 photograph in The Burn. Loggers were faced with an unprecedented tangle of deteriorating logs and debris.

Photo by Darius Kinsey *Courtesy Washington County Historical Museum*

Above: The huge logging-lumbering camp of Consolidated Timber Company at Glenwood, northwest of Forest Grove, was a brawling highball center of salvage operations. Millions of board feet flowed through the big camp, to be processed at local sawmills or sent by rail or truck to other mills. The fire-ridden forest, where one of the fires began, was just up the Gales Creek Canyon, barely visible in the background. Shops are in center of picture. A long logging train winds up the draw, a working steam locomotive on the adjacent track.

Photo by Darius Kinsey *Courtesy Bert Pickens*

Right: The famed Pacific Northwest logging photographer, Darius Kinsey, was invited to Consolidated Camp to record the tremendous salvage operation. He lined up the crew at a typical salvage logging show (save for one logger who turned his back on them near the spar pole). Shown are Pete Branda, Glen Paulson, Chris Benner, Jack Ramsey, Mike Hall, Fay Seehorn, Curley Williams, Lee Lockett, Jack Reeder, Harley Case, and Bert Pickens.

Photo by Darius Kinsey   Courtesy Bert Pickens

Another salvage show of Consolidated Timber's. Loggers loved to pose for the camera. Their outfits were typical of the times — tin pants, heavy shirts, calked boots, and the inevitable red hats.

Below: To move out the salvage timber, Consolidated spent some $1.5 million in the deep years of the Great Depression for a vast network of railroads and equipment. More was expended for truck roads. These salvage logs are heading for a mill. Much of the timber was sound, despite its appearance.

Photo by Darius Kinsey   Courtesy Bert Pickens

Some areas were virtually unsalvageable, such as this one strewn with black logs and heavy with ash. No new life is showing up here. Some sections were so badly burned and re-burned, and the fires so hot, that nothing could grow.

Driving through The Burn was often like traveling through a forest of the dead. After a few years, black snags were bleached by the summer sun and were a familiar sight to Oregonians. In the background, snags have been felled from a hillside in the Kilchis area. A fire lookout post is visible on the ridge.

Courtesy Southern Pacific

This incline logging railroad, with an 80 percent grade, was among the more spectacular logging shows, believed to be at the Blue Star Camp near Enright. Legend has it that a loaded car of logs once broke loose, took out the Tillamook main line, and shot clear across the Salmonberry River Canyon. Edwards Logging Company spent $200 thousand to build the spur and passing track near Enright. The big fire wiped out the spur and the company.

Left: It appears that this hillside has been thoroughly scoured. Some growth is coming back. Many small logging operations were scattered through the Tillamook Burn Country, using traditional steam donkeys like this one.

Photo by Ellis Lucia

In any man's language, the Tillamook Burn was rugged country. In later years another steep incline spur of 22 percent was working at Belding, by Gilmore Logging. The heavy flat cars of logs were slowly let down to the main line by donkey and cable, visible in the lower left corner.

A long pole train pauses at Cochran, headed for sawmills along the Willamette River and in the Tualatin Valley. Trains like this were a familiar sight during salvage years, when the Tillamook branch of the Southern Pacific played an integral part in the salvage operation. The line ran in rugged, isolated backcountry through the heart of The Burn. (See Chapter V.)

Photo by Ellis Lucia

Sketched by D. M. Swain from an old photo by Ellis Lucia

Reeher's Camp was established near Cochran under the Civilian Conservation Corps program of the 1930s. Thousands of young men, mainly from the South and the East, found a new life in the Tillamook Burn during the Great Depression years. Legend has it that this was where Oregon's possum population began, the animals being brought in by southern CCC boys. Reeher's Camp (which had no connection with the Reeher family) miraculously escaped the great fire. Later it fell into disarray, only occasionally used by foresters. For a time it was considered a possible site for a trusty camp of the Oregon Penitentiary, but this idea was rejected because of location and crumbling structures.

Thousands of CCC boys were located in camps fringing the Tillamook Burn. They fought fires, worked in the cleanup, and later planted trees. The only death in the Big Fire was that of Frank Palmer, a CCC member from Illinois. A tree fell on him while he was resting. Many CCC boys who fought in the 1933 holocaust had never faced a forest fire and were unaware of its dangers. The group here is from Camp Trask.

Courtesy Oregon Historical Society

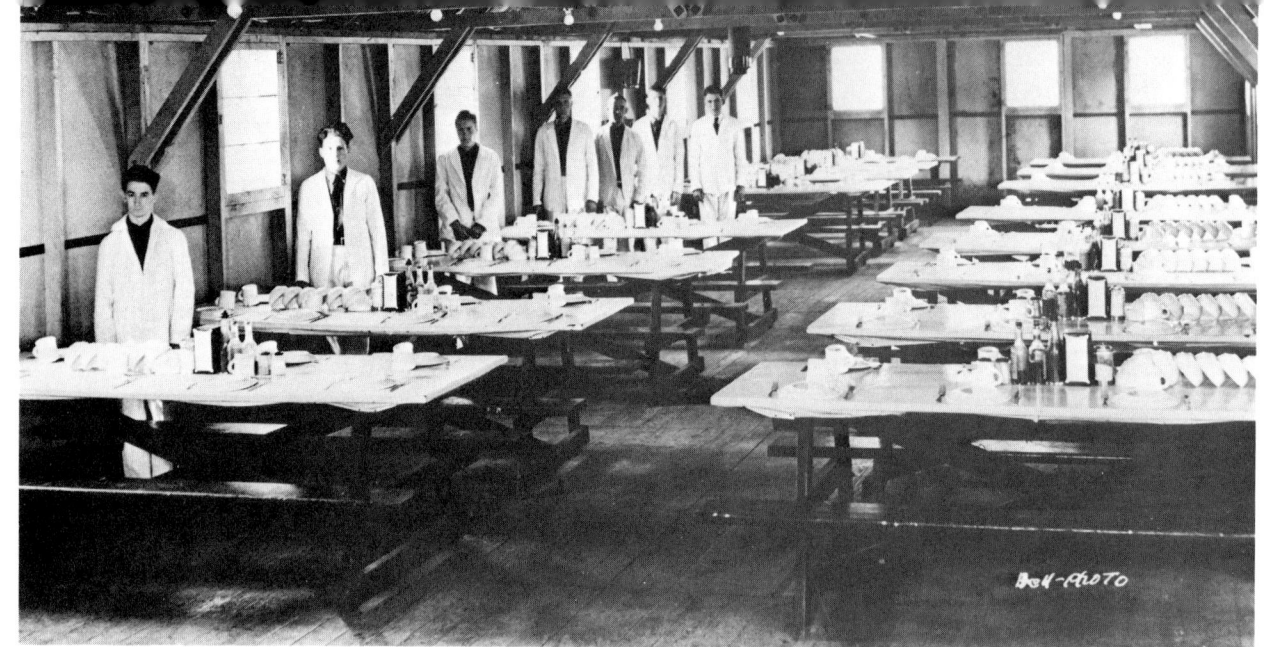

Courtesy Oregon Historical Society

Accommodations for the federal government's CCC program were good and spotless. Even critics of Franklin D. Roosevelt's New Deal admitted that it was a fine program. This is the dining room at Camp Nehalem. Reeher's Camp was much the same before it fell into disuse.

The "Three Cs," as they were often called, did a lot to improve state and federal forests, not only in Oregon but throughout the country. Thousands of young men worked and learned in the outdoors and furnished a ready backup source of fire fighters. They built trails and established camping and picnic areas. On weekends they flooded beach resort communities like Seaside on the Tillamook Burn fringe, where they took over the roller rink. Many boys were from big eastern cities; living in the wilds was a new experience. The draft and Pearl Harbor killed the program, with the boys going into service.

Courtesy Southern Pacific

In the great salvage years a tangled network of railroads covered The Burn and much of northwestern Oregon. The rugged terrain made geared locomotives a necessity.

Courtesy Oregon Historical Society

Photos by Ellis Lucia
Logging The Burn also required trestles everywhere, with so many draws and canyons. A few still stand as examples of a bygone age and are curiosities for tourists.

The Never-Still roundhouse was just what its name implied. Locomotives, cars, and other equipment were repaired at this center north of the main Tillamook Burn. Finally abandoned, the roundhouse has stood for years as a landmark to logging.

Photo by Curtis Nesheim

Oregon-American, which had a huge mill at Vernonia, moved salvage from the ridges and canyons by rail in the northern portion of The Burn, south of the Sunset Highway.

Photo by Curtis Nesheim

Oregon-American acquired its locomotive from Long-Bell, then got so busy nobody ever had time to change the name on the tender. Long-Bell took salvage from another portion of The Burn, but used trucks. This scene was at Kesey.

Not all the salvage was scrap, by any means. There was much sound old growth like these huge logs. Some trees escaped the flames or received a once-over-lightly.

Courtesy John Coats

Logging operators used a variety of equipment to loft and skid the downed timber off the slopes. Steam was being replaced by gas and diesel rigs, marking the beginning of a full-scale revolution of all phases of the timber industry, some of which had its inception in the Tillamook Burn.

Courtesy John Coats

Unlike logging a standing forest, working the Tillamook was at times a weird operation. This was rough country, with steep slopes and high ridges. Trying to sort out the good and bad timber took much doing, yet many gypos and larger independent operators acquired cleanup contracts from the counties and private land holders.

Courtesy John Coats

Gradually power saws, heavy and large, began to appear in the Tillamook Burn, the last conversion from muscle power. This was the layout of Coats Logging Company, back from the Wilson River. Salvage logging moved on both sides of the summit.

Courtesy John Coats

Salvage loggers worked with timber that in years gone by would have been left on the ground, like this splintered piece. Buckers are using an electric or compressed-air power saw (note cord on left). Misery whips and springboards were also still in use during these years.

Courtesy John Coats

Salvaged logs are skidded by Cat to loading site. Snags and rubble appear in background.

Amid rubble, truck is being loaded for haul to the Coats sawmill at Tillamook. These timbers appear to be sounder than many salvage sticks.

Courtesy John Coats

103

Courtesy John Coats

Left: Heavy logging trucks streamed along major highways night and day from The Burn country to the coastal communities of Seaside, Tillamook, and Astoria, and to inland towns such as Forest Grove, Hillsboro, Carlton, and McMinnville. These Mack trucks are bound for a Tillamook sawmill.

Courtesy John Coats

Below: The Coats sawmill at Tillamook processed much salvage timber, beginning soon after the 1933 fire, as did many mills ringing the wasteland. Coats lumbering was a family tradition from the days of tall ships, some of which were owned by the company.

Photo by Ellis Lucia
Left: Small and large sawmills had long been into logging and lumbering. This pioneer enterprise of the Pacific Northwest began with the Hudson's Bay mill on the Columbia, up-river from Fort Vancouver. That mill was the first to ship cut lumber overseas. This typical small mill was near The Burn. Many ranches had sawmills.

Photos by Ellis Lucia
Below: From the 1930s into the mid-1950s, rustic sawmills encircled The Burn. Their clatter was heard around the clock. Working in the woods and mills was a leading endeavor for husky youths and adult males. The mills architecture was of a wide variety. Chilling winds blew right through them, and if they caught fire, they burned fast and hot.

Photo above by Ellis Lucia

Old-style sawmilling was utilitarian and, like the early blacksmiths, a trade that was fading. Sawyers at the head rigs judged the cuts with a practiced eye and used hand signals. Mills like this are a far cry from today's well-lighted plants with their computerized equipment.

Photo by Allan J. de Lay

"Peggy" worked many years in The Burn, running to Camp Murphy. Later she was used in the yard of Stimson's sawmill, hauling salvage lumber. The author well remembers seeing her there. The 1909 Shay, later retired, was given to the Forestry Building, and survived the 1964 fire which destroyed the huge log cabin from the Lewis and Clark World's Fair. Today "Peggy" stands near the Western Forestry Center in Portland.

Photo by Fred H. Lemcke *Courtesy Fritz Photos*

Stimson's huge sawmill operation in Scoggins Valley, southwest of Forest Grove, was on the edge of The Burn. The firm owned its land and salvaged much timber in the vicinity. The company moved south from Seattle.

Diamond Lumber Company's logging and sawmill operation stood in the heart of The Burn (*center of photo*) surrounded by the rugged, fire-devastated mountains. Roy Gould was famous as an energetic operator who took contracts from Tillamook County at a dollar a thousand board feet. In the years of the Great Depression, loggers were paid about forty or forty-five cents an hour and were charged a dollar for a bed and seventy-five cents a day for meals.

Black logs kept coming off the steep slopes for years and were amazingly free of deterioration. Unhappily, minor and major fires continued to plague the great wasteland, destroying additional timber and new trees.

This crew did salvage logging and operated a sm[all] railroad in the heart of the Tillamook Burn. Many [of] the loggers were young.

Courtesy Washington County Historical Mus[eum]

Photo by Ellis Lucia
A hint of things to come, this little sawmill used in the Tillamook Burn was "portable." These loggers/lumbermen cut boards right on the spot. When ready to move, the mill was hoisted onto a logging truck. Thus it was possible to work over the small material. Wartime and postwar high prices encouraged the cleanup for more than two decades after the big fire. The condition also delayed reforestation, as owners refused to give up their lands.

For many years, the salvage logging trucks were a familiar sight on roads and highways. While a welcome sign of industry, the impact was felt in other ways in towns like Forest Grove, where the big rigs lined up at the main intersection for a wide swing left. Sometimes they didn't make it. Laws were overlooked, especially in wartime; trucks were overloaded, or their few bind chains would break, causing disaster.

Heavily loaded log trucks might suddenly let go of their loads, smashing everything. This one took out highway signs. The "No U Turn" seems incongruous. Sometimes cars were flattened, and more than one death resulted. Following World War II, laws were strengthened on load limits and chain binding. Truck operators had claimed that it was more profitable to pay fines for overloads than to make more hauls.

Forest Grove had a particularly serious problem with salvage log and lumber trucks headed directly into town from Gales Creek and Glenwood. A whipping curve and grade caused them to drop loads directly in front of a grade school. Sometimes logs rolled across the lawn, almost to the front door. Fortunately, it never happened when youngsters were around. But an enterprising principal and teachers kept a record of the "lost teaching time" from trucks shifting gears to make the grade, and the cost to taxpayers. Truck drivers promised to be more careful rounding the curve. The case was made; the route was changed away from school.

Fire wasn't limited to the wasteland of the Tillamook country. During the great salvage years, many a sawmill caught fire, only to be patched up and put back into action. This hot one was at Carnation Mill in the early 1950s. Another was a sudden blaze at the Larkins sawmill. Carnation, a major mill, lost no time in rebuilding *(right)*.

The railroads took the timbers down to splash in the bays, inlets, and rivers, to be boomed up, and floated to the mills. During the war years salvage work reached a crescendo.

Whopping logs like this one, about to be dumped near Astoria, were hauled from The Burn region. Highways carried a steady parade of timbers bound for the many sawmills. Among the largest in later years was a pair from the Wilson River country by Purdin Logging Company; ten feet in diameter, eighteen feet long, and each containing about 6,300 board feet.

Courtesy Oregon Historical Society

Scenes similar to this were commonplace throughout the Tillamook Burn Country, from the Columbia River south to Tillamook and McMinnville and inland to the Willamette River. This was the Hammon Mill at Astoria.

Courtesy Oregon Historical Society

Great quantities of Tillamook Burn timber went directly into the war effort to build the shipyards in Portland and for keels of subchasers and mine sweepers. Oddly, the timber was doomed to burn later, when the shipyards caught fire at the war's end. Following the war, the spacious blimp hangers at Tillamook, used for submarine patrol of the coastline, became plywood and sawmill plants, operated by the invincible Roy Gould. In the 1980s, a hanger was used to develop a dirigible-style logging airlift.

Courtesy Mrs. Alf C. Johannesen/ELC

The tremendous wartime effort of Consolidated Timber Company earned the coveted Army-Navy E Award, presented September 23, 1943, at the huge Glenwood Camp, under wartime security. Military braid was on hand for the outdoor ceremony. A sixty-piece brass band for Fort Stevens, near Astoria, played, and luncheon followed in the spacious logging camp dining hall. That appears to be Dr. Walter C. Giersbach, president of Pacific University, at the rostrum, giving the invocation as the audience stands. A disinterested cook leans against the door frame, his back to the ceremony.

Courtesy Mrs. Alf C. Johannesen/ELC

Below: Serving as master of ceremonies, Orville R. Miller, representing the industry, outlined wartime achievements. At far right is Lloyd R. Crosby, Consolidated manager who put together The Burn's huge salvage operation. On his right is John W. Blodgett, Jr., president of Consolidated.

Courtesy Mrs. Alf C. Johannesen/ELC

Lapel pins with the letter E went to workers from many segments of the Consolidated operations. Mrs. Rila Snyder and Judson James represented company employees; Worth Lowery, organized labor and the IWW. Alf C. Johannesen receives his pin from Lt. Comdr. H. N. Anderson, U.S. Naval Reserve, from the Navy lumber procurement office in Portland. Many loggers wore the pins.

The large Army-Navy E banner would fly proudly over the camp. The wartime citation was given to industries for their high production efforts to defeat Hitler and the Japanese. From left: John W. Blodgett, Jr.; Col. Fred G. Sherrill, Corps of Engineers, Washington, D.C.; Orville R. Miller; Lt. Comdr. H. N. Anderson; and Lloyd R. Crosby.

Courtesy Mrs. Alf C. Johannesen/ELC

Following the war, only a few good years remained for major logging on a wide scale in The Burn. Consolidated closed operations in the early 1950s, and the camp was later converted to a trolley museum and park. Railroad hobbyists took over the right-of-way from Banks to Vernonia for summer passenger trains. The end of an era was close at hand.

Symbolic of the finale to old-time logging and lumbering was the 1964 burning of the historic Forestry Building in northwest Portland. Billed as "the world's largest log cabin," the massive structure was erected by loggers for the 1905 Lewis and Clark World's Fair.

Chapter Five

THE HUSKY BRANCH LINE

"It was a spectacular sight . . . five or six locomotives . . . all blasted along with widened throttles . . . pillars of smoke belched skyward from this collection of power as the train snailed up the crooked track, rarely over fifteen miles an hour."

George Abdill

As RAILROADS GO, the line to the Oregon coast across the wild, on-end country known as the Tillamook Burn ranks high on the list as both rugged and awesome. Railroaders still call it the P.R. & N. and by a dubious nickname: the Punk, Rotten and Nasty, which about sums it up. Yet this tough, wheeling branch, which for two decades was traveled by thousands of beach lovers on "Suntan Specials," became a vital factor in the effort to salvage the timber devastated by the several Tillamook fires.

The line had first been envisioned by E. E. Lytle, a prominent railroad builder after the turn of the century. Track laying began under the name Pacific Railway & Navigation Company and by 1906 was as far as Buxton, a tiny community on the fringes of the great forest. It would be six years before the line could run trains to the coast; the railroaders were facing mountain barriers that were almost insurmountable. They had to drill eleven tunnels, erect innumerable high trestles, and span deep canyons at dizzying heights. By then Lytle had gone broke in the panic of 1907. He sold the line to E. H. Harriman, who completed the track and operated the line for a number of years. Later, it came into the fold of the Southern Pacific, which still maintains the branch with freights running several times weekly.

The holocaust of 1933 knocked out the system for weeks, burning and weakening tunnels and trestles. Yet when salvage logging gained momentum, and for much of the next three decades, the P.R. & N. was a mainstay in hauling millions of board feet out of the deep Salmonberry River canyon and across the Tualatin Valley floor to a log dump at Menefee on the Willamette River. Little Timber, which somehow had escaped the fires, was turned into a busy railroad center for pulling the heavy pole trains up the hill to the 1,806-foot summit and 800-foot rise between Timber and Cochran, over 2 and 3 percent grades and 18-degree curves. And, in peak years, about 90 percent of the rail traffic was timber.

In the late 1940s, the Southern Pacific started phasing out its steam locomotives, replacing them with less colorful but more efficient diesel power. This turned Timber into almost a ghost town. It was in the late summer of 1950 that, as a newspaper feature writer raised in a railroad town, I made a memorable trip over the old P.R. & N. to view the changes and hear the legends. The first change was peering into the empty Timber roundhouse, with not a steamer in sight.

Courtesy Douglas County Museum

In what was always high drama, six steam locomotives huff and puff a long, mixed train up the great sweeping horseshoe of Wolf Creek, three on the front at left, three on the rear end far below at right, followed by a caboose. Heavily loaded cars of logs extend from the front end through a tunnel. This picture was taken in the early 1940s of a sight seldom seen by the general public.

A beach train from the coast halts at Cochran, the line's 1,806-foot summit, to be checked over, its four locomotives panting like prehistoric monsters. This was the second section of a G.A.R. (Grand Army of the Republic) excursion, indicating the popularity of the line. Timber was heavy then. The trains snaked at fifteen miles an hour through many miles of dark tunnels made by trees, where passengers could touch the branches. Wildlife was often seen close at hand. Huge crosscut saws stood in the ends of the cars. When heavy storms swept the woods, blowdowns fell across the tracks, and passengers joined crews clearing the way. Regular passenger service ended in the 1930s when the Wilson River Highway was opened. Train riders found the Astoria-Seaside route quicker for beach weekends.

Courtesy Douglas County Museum

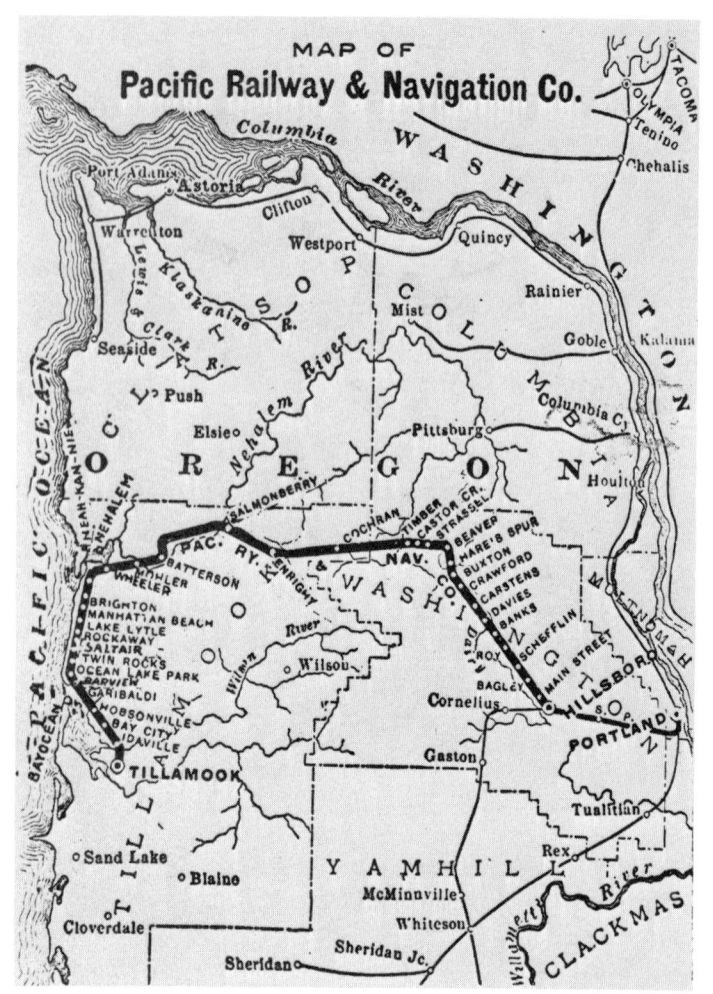

Courtesy Douglas County Museum

Left: An early-day map shows the route of the P.R. & N. railroad, connecting Portland and Tillamook. The line linked many Tualatin Valley villages and those in the mountains and on the coast.

Below: About to leave Tillamook, this steam train is bound for Portland. A single locomotive was sufficient along the coast and into the back country. Additional engines joined at Batterson's passing track. Regular passenger service ended in the early 1930s when the Wilson River Highway was opened. Train riders found the Astoria-Seaside route quicker for weekenders.

Courtesy Southern Pacific

Courtesy Southern Pacific

SP 2001 (4-6-0) waits on a siding for a train, shortly after the line was opened in 1911–12. Locomotives first burned wood, which was certainly in quantity; later they switched to diesel oil.

Courtesy Douglas County Museum

Another extra 2825 waits at Cochran. Railroad crews were constantly shuttling the steamers up or down the steep grades between Timber, Cochran, and the lower Salmonberry River.

Courtesy Southern Pacific

Timber was proud of its unusual log depot, one of few in the nation, with its stone fireplace. The milk cans are ready for the next train. Locomotive was of 1907 vintage, 4-8-0, class TW-3. It was scrapped in November 1949.

Courtesy Southern Pacific

Snow was often heavy in the Coast Range. At times it was difficult to keep the railroad open, as this engine is discovering against a backdrop of thick, snowy forest.

Being high in the mountains, Timber often bore the brunt of winter storms which almost buried railroad buildings and isolated the little town.

By the turn of the decade into the 1950s, diesel power had retired the aging steam locomotives. The passenger trains were gone — and so were the trees. The P.R. & N. remained a vigorous freight line, much of it devoted to hauling salvage timber.

Diesel locomotives like this striper could bring a heavy train of logs up the mountainside much more easily than the steamers. Three 1,500-horsepower diesels could do the work of five steam engines. This view and others in this sequence were made a few months after the changeover took place.

The steep corkscrew mountain line required constant equipment checking, locomotives and cars like. Archie Archambault, who came to the Tillamook branch in 1923, checked the trains wherever they paused, for the line was tough on running gear.

About all that was left of Cochran, hard hit by the original fire, was the railroad station and water tower. Cochran was once a thriving mill town, too; the Wheeler sawmill operated there. It was destroyed by the fire, leaving only the millpond. P.R. & N. served eleven logging operations and 155 sawmills.

A steady flow of salvage timber went inland from the Tillamook Burn through this treeless country during World War II and postwar years. This long pole train, as they were called, is headed for Timber and then east perhaps to a dump at Menafee, near Portland, about sixty miles away.

The picturesque log depot at Timber stood for about another decade but burned in the late 1950s. In right background, the huge roundhouse is visible. As many as ten steam locomotives had gathered there, but now it was empty. From Timber to Cochran Summit, the railroad climbed more than eight hundred feet in seven miles and underwent a rigid safety check before sliding down the other side.

This old water tower has reached the end of the line, along with other buildings. In the greatest years 90 percent of the P.R. & N. traffic was logs. In 1956 the car total was 1,049 cars, for an accumulated gross revenue of $40,105. By 1957 the total had dropped dramatically to 77 cars and $4,741, while in the first five months of 1958 the station handled only seven carloads, with gross revenue of $1,847. Although the railroad continued to haul through-freight to the coast, Espee decided to close the station agency. It spelled the end of Timber as a vigorous railroad center and was clearly the finale of the salvage years.

An aging commuter car from southern California serves as a combination caboose and passenger car, since the line was still carrying riders into the backcountry, retaining its status as a mixed train. Conductor George Humphrey, veteran railroader of over forty years, stands in the doorway.

Ed Fink (*center*) was assigned the line to instruct crews in the care and feeding of diesel locomotives, as opposed to steam. He chats with Dave Redman, fireman, and N. Tate, head brakeman. Trainmaster Sam Burton is on the left. The rugged line took special training.

Bill Rufner worked for the P.R. & N. as a diesel engineer during these crucial salvage years. Leonard Kendall was rear brakeman. Dave Hall was also a member of the crew as swing brakeman.

Business was still being conducted as it always had been, by telegraph and sturdy upright typewriter. The crew also used hand and air signals, as radio contact hadn't yet come to the line.

The hills were bare of trees in this isolated, lonely backcountry. Vine maple grew profusely, turning a fiery red in autumn. It appears that snags had been felled and some salvage done along this hillside.

Crewman tosses rolled paper from train window to waiting dog, who catches it and takes it to his master. This was a daily ritual.

Among those who hated towns and liked backcountry living without telephones or a car was Tony Savage, who had a little farm deep in Salmonberry Canyon. His dog met the train and brought his paper and mail to him. During heavy winters, railroad crews checked on the welfare of backcountry folk and brought them supplies.

With its steep grades and wheeling curves, riding a scooter into the canyon was like an amusement park roller coaster. The line needed constant inspection and repair; sometimes railroaders had to "join the birds" on a derailment.

Gandy dancers replace weakened heavy-duty rail, for this is mountain railroading. Without scheduled passenger trains, if a freight jumped the track on Friday night, the crew sometimes walked out, waiting 'til Monday to pick up the pieces.

The line twisted along one side of the narrow canyon, with Salmonberry River on the left. Bleached snags high above gleam in the sun, and only a few trees survive for natural reforestation.

For miles, the Salmonberry Canyon is nearly sheer bluffs, bleak and foreboding. Few people even today, traveling modern highways to the Oregon Coast, realize how rugged is this section of the Coast Range.

Gilmore Logging, in an act of daring, operated a 100-yard spur on a 22 percent grade to a loading boom. A donkey engine with a cable attached to a flatcar lets the loads down the steep grade to the main line siding for pickup. When the cable played out, the car traveled the remaining distance, braked by a logger with a crowbar, running alongside and turning the brake wheel.

Sharpness of the grade is clearly visible, and the holding donkey cable may be seen at left. Runaways were known to knock out the main line. Loaded cars had no safety chains; sometimes logs dropped off during the run to Cochran and beyond. When enough were strewn along the line, a special train with a crane was dispatched to pick up the sticks.

Logging operations had sidings all along the route in the lower river canyon, at Enright, Batterson, Salmonberry, Mohler, and other points. Spaulding Pulp & Paper operated this one at Mohler, loading six cars a day. The train used gondola cars as well as open flatcars. Most were bound to inland sawmills; a westbound train returned with empties.

Courtesy Southern Pacific

Photo by Tom McAllister

Loggers, anglers, and hunters often rode the rattlers into this backcountry, away from the pressures of too many sportsmen. Later, foresters joined them. Salmonberry was an excellent stream for winter steelheading.

Photo by Tom McAllister

A Portland attorney, Bill Shurtz, maintained a retreat hunting lodge in the heart of The Burn, about halfway down the Salmonberry. The only way in or out was via the railroad, but it was a paradise for sportsmen.

In those years the vast, open Tillamook Burn was great deer country. Tom McAllister examines a fine four-point blacktail buck shot at close range. A storm raged along the snaggy ridgetops.

Photo by Tom McAllister

A track walker named Mark helped Bill Shurtz load the deer into a scooter for the trip back up to Timber. Just where the hunters would ride to operate the scooter is a good guess. Two decades later, as the forest began coming back, the deer population started declining. Not all hunters were happy to see the trees growing tall.

Photo by Tom McAllister

Photo by Ellis Lucia

There were occasional arguments about right-of-away

Photo by Ellis Lucia
A few steam locomotives were still running along the Tillamook branch in the early 1950s, at least in the valley flatlands. Old 2853 had the last word against the diesels on a snowy day, smacking a farmer's truck. So much for the Age of Steam.

Chapter Six

THE ANGRY SCAR

"We are just a little burned up at the way the program has been handled in the past. We don't think it has been handled. We're going to have a fire in another few years because nothing has been done about it, and nothing is going to be done about it."

Judge Harland M. Wood

UNLESS YOU SAW the Tillamook Burn firsthand from a high ridge on a clear day, you couldn't imagine how bad it really was. Or how tremendous in size. It seemed to go on forever, in ever direction.

In the early decades of this century, the Pacific Northwest had suffered many great forest fires of substantial size. But the Tillamook Burn disaster was different. Instead of being secluded far back in the mountains, it was right up front, for all to see. It was only forty miles from Oregon's largest population center, Portland, and was traversed by two major highways to the state's popular northern beaches. Motorists got a close, firsthand view of The Burn's bleached snags and rubble each time they traveled the Wilson River and Sunset highways.

This was also an age when proud Oregonians placed great importance on the natural beauty of their state and were developing a tourist industry that would become international. Moreover, timber was running out in what was purportedly among the finest regions on the continent for growing healthy big trees.

The Tillamook Burn was well on the way to becoming a vast wasteland which might not come back naturally for centuries. As World War II wound down and people again focused their interests on home affairs, Oregonians wanted something done. It was more than just talk; it was a grassroots movement to clean up the mess and bring back the big woods.

The groundwork had been laid in the early forties, while war was raging in Europe and the Far East. Governor Earl Snell appointed a special committee to study The Burn problem, headed by Judge H. D. Kerkman of Washington County. There were many hearings which, if nothing else, helped stir discussion among the people on the streets, and in bars and taverns. There was also the constant reminder that The Burn was just beyond the hills, in the smoke-filled air from slash fires and occasional runaways, and the many sawmills surrounding the northwest Oregon region. The logging trucks streamed along the roadways and through the towns, and I have seen them many times stacked up five and six trucks deep on Main Street in Forest Grove, like the trolley iron monsters on San Francisco's Market Street, waiting to make the precarious swing onto Pacific Avenue to head east.

Oregonians realized, too, that negative talk was in the wind and a consideration of easy solutions. A major article in the Sunday Magazine section of the state's leading newspaper suggested turning The Burn to grass and range lands. Then, there was that study by the U.S. Forest Service. . . . The hearings reflected discouragement over the problem and a tendency to give up. The idea of seeding to grasslands for range was branded as ridiculous, since the area was far too rugged for either cattle or cowboys. Its prime value, as I have said before, was in the growing of big, fat, tremendous trees in quantity.

In those years, there was little discussion of getting the forest back to restore the wildlife and birds. Assuredly, local folk wanted it, because being so close to such a wilderness had been a major pleasure of living in Oregon. You could count on a limit of trout, salmon and winter steelhead, and your deer and elk in season. There were the birds . . . the wild flowers . . . the berries . . . the woodland hikes . . . the fresh air. . . . But these things came in the natural course of events, so that few voiced any concern in the lush Oregon Country over the ecology, or even knew what the word meant, and Pacific Northwest with its small population had the greatest environment in the world.

What had happened to eastern cities could never happen here, except in the distant minds of a few visionaries like Stewart Holbrook, the great timber author, who created his own private campaign, known as the James G. Blaine Association, to "keep and discourage people from moving to Oregon." The only other local groups which foresaw serious trouble if The Burn wasn't restored were city and county officials who wondered where future water resources for their communities would come from. And of course, there were the deer hunters who secretly wanted to keep The Burn as it now was — some of the greatest deer hunting country in the West, if not the nation.

It is something of a wonder that all the factions ever got together at all, and it is to their credit that they did. They took the gamble to reforest The Burn, and in the process changed forestry, logging and environmental history.

Photo by Kirk Braun   *Ellis Lucia Collection*

A lookout keeps his vigil over one of the strangest forests on the continent, largely of snags. Fire, from whatever source, remained The Burn's foremost problem, a major reason the trees wouldn't come back.

Photo by Hugh Ackroyd

The snags were thick in places, even after the years of salvage, along steep hillsides and deep ravines. This scene was south of the Sunset Highway. It appears that fire has been burning here.

Courtesy OSFD, USFS
Ellis Lucia Collection

The Tillamook Burn problem was mind-boggling, as people say today. Its staggering size and scope show the armies of snags, the ruggedness of the land, and how void it appeared of foliage and regrowth. The area was about 350,000 acres, with a 500,000-acre problem area, stretching through four counties. The disaster changed lives, the economy, and — some said — even the weather.

Photo by Curtis Nesheim
Almost as threatening and destructive as fire were wood-boring worms like this rascal. Despite the early massive salvage operation, much sound timber remained — if bugs and disease didn't get there first.

Feeble efforts were made toward reforestation even in the ear thirties, following the big fire. Boys of the Civilian Conservatic Corps (CCC) went on planting sojourns and also worked at clea up and road building. But The Burn was so huge that plantin were little more than a pinprick, and successive fires might d stroy the young trees. There was also the problem of securi seedlings.

The pioneer Reeher family, who had retained their homestead on the Wilson River, organized their own tree-planting expeditions, one of the first among private citizens. It was a demonstration of what many people felt. In 1946 the Reehers planted five thousand trees and the following year eight thousand. The Reehers cherished the tall timber and its beauty. What happened became a personal dedication. In all, they planted one hundred thousand seedlings.

Courtesy Mildred S. Reeher

Courtesy Oregon Historical Society

Youth groups took up the cause, many of them under the supervision of State Forester Nelson S. Rogers, who was raised at Gales Creek and well remembered the old forest. These high school boys from Timber, Hillsboro, and Forest Grove in 1945 planted forty thousand Port Orford seedlings along an 8½-mile strip of the Wilson River Highway. For some, this was their second year under a four-year "beautification program."

Beach-bound Oregonians by the thousands, and their tourist visitors, traveled through the heart of The Burn. The sight wasn't to their liking. The location of The Burn became a major factor in a ground-swell movement for rehabilitation. This is the Wilson River route, with Kings Mountain in the background.

141

Courtesy Oregon Historical Society

Periodically, events were staged and publicized to keep the interest alive, such as this tree-planting by State Forester Nelson S. Rogers (with shovel). Also shown, from left, are Cecil Kyle, chief warden for the Northwest Forest Protective Association at the time of the '33 fire; Arthur W. Priaulx, in charge of public relations for the powerful West Coast Lumbermen's Association; and Lynn S. Cronemiller, state forester on the '33 holocaust.

In 1943, while war still raged throughout the world, State Forester Nels Rogers *(left)* came up with a solid plan for rehabilitating The Burn. Gov. Earl Snell endorsed the plan and appointed a special forestry committee, headed by Judge H. D. Kerkman of Washington County, to study the course of action. The committee recommended a bond issue, but the scope of the problem might result in pouring good money after badlands.

Photo by Thomas C. Adams   *Courtesy USFS*

The dream of Nels Rogers was the return of the forest of his youth in Vernonia and Gales Creek, where the trees were dense and grand, the wildlife happy. There were small reminders on the rim, but beyond . . .

Many of the state's editors had their reservations, but Editor-Publisher Hugh McGilvra *(left)* launched his own crusade to bring The Burn back to life. Fresh out of college, McGilvra had purchased the *Washington County News-Times* only four years before disaster struck. A staunch advocate and believer in movements from the grass roots, McGilvra wrote editorial after editorial favoring a full-scale rehabilitation program. These were reprinted around the state and helped alter public postwar thinking. The author *(right)* was assigned to cover The Burn. Edna Martin, now with the *Medford Mail-Tribune,* was also a staffer on the key country weekly.

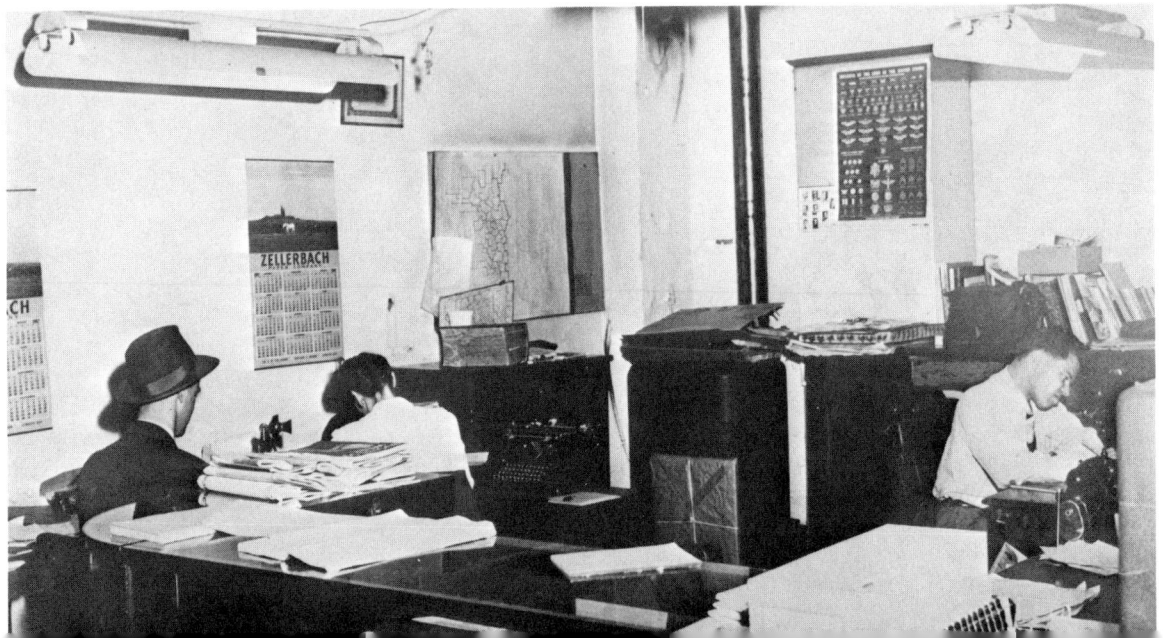

Sketched by D. M. Swain from photograph in Ellis Lucia Collection

A large newspaper feature in the statewide Northwest Magazine of *The Oregonian* advocated turning Oregon's forest fire-devastated areas into "rangeland" for cattle and sheep. The Burn was already moving in that direction, with cattle and horses roaming over the high-speed Sunset Highway, causing innumerable accidents before the Oregon State Highway Department got around to posting Open Range warning signs. A local grange then changed the law in the state legistature, fixing responsibility on livestock owners.

Opening of the Sunset Highway and the earlier Wilson River route just before World War II gave Oregonians a firsthand look at this great scar as they burst through the Sunset Tunnel by the thousands on their way to the beach, especially after completion of a cutoff from Banks to Portland. The highway, formerly called the Wolf Creek, was renamed in honor of Oregon's heroic Sunset Division of the National Guard in World War II and not because it traveled into the sunset, as many people still believe.

Photo by Fred H. ("Fritz") Lemcke
The state was quietly acquiring timberlands in the Tillamook Burn Country through the counties, as they became available for taxes. As manpower grew in the postwar years, fire crews were increased. The Oregon State Forestry Department conducted special fire schools to train suppression crews in the northwest district. John Doran, district forester, explains firefighting techniques on an actual controlled fire.

Photo by Fred H. ("Fritz") Lemcke
The fire-fighting schools, staged all around the state, gave greenhorns both classroom and actual field training, everything from handling tools to reading maps and using shortwave radios and trailing actual fires. In the northwest district, these pioneering schools, conducted by experienced foresters like John Doran, were especially important. Making the Tillamook Burn fireproof was the prime requisite of any effort to bring back the woods.

Crystal Mitchell for years trained lookouts who would keep rigid watch on The Burn. Among them was Chet Cunningham, who spent several summers on an isolated lookout trying to become a writer. Later he authored many fiction and nonfiction books in southern California. (See Chapter X.)

The war had developed much lightweight equipment, which shortly became available to civilians and state and local departments. Lightweight, compact radios for the field were one item, power saws another. These portable pumps are compared by Tom Seth, warehouseman, and Bob Burke, mechanic, for use in The Burn. The large pump weighed one hundred pounds; the newer type, only thirty-eight.

Fires from one cause or another continued to harass any plan for rehabilitation, like this one on Green Mountain. The 1945 blowup almost broke the private Northwest Forest Protective Association. As state foresters moved in, they built up equipment and organized suppression crews to hit any outbreak fast and hard. In October 1945 the Oregon State Board of Forestry canceled its contract with the association and assumed direct responsibility for protecting The Burn.

Resembling the set for the popular television Show M*A*S*H of later years, foresters established a base operation at the Owl Camp, once a logging railroad center at the summit of the Wilson River Highway. Through the years, it became a rendezvous center for Tillburn activities and ceremonies. It was renamed Rogers Camp for Nelson Rogers, who died when his program was only beginning.

Public meetings about The Burn were held throughout the state. Many were at the Owl Camp, both before and after reforestation was launched. The 1947 state legislature submitted a constitutional amendment for a bond issue not to exceed 0.75 percent of Oregon's assessed valuation. Voters approved it unhesitatingly in the November 1948 general election, making $10.5 million available. This Owl Camp gathering is listening to discussion about The Burn. Seated on the left are Judge H. D. Kerkman, Washington County, who headed the Snell forestry committee; and Hugh McGilvra, editor-publisher at Forest Grove, who pushed for complete reforestation. Other key county judges working with Kerkman were Guy Boyington of Clatsop County and Harlan M. Wood of Tillamook County.

There was nothing very formal about these meetings, but the county officials and public-spirited citizens were determined. In the background, as former State Forester Lynn S. Cronemiller spoke, was the staunch reminder of the barren, snag-infested hills.

Dignitaries sat on chunks of wood amid clutter of the Owl Camp, eating lunch and listening to R. M. ("Rudy") Kallander *(facing camera)*, who was picked to lead the program as rehabilitation director. To his left is John Wood, Sr., who would handle the collecting of seed cones, vital to replanting in the early years.

All along there had been pressure to turn The Burn into grasslands, but this seemed a waste. Valley towns were concerned about their watersheds and, through a cooperative effort, were planting trees; 250,000 Douglas fir and Port Orford seedlings had been set out in the vicinity of Cochran and the old Reeher's CCC camp. H. D. Kerkman, Washington County judge, and acting State Forester George Spaur describe the progress as slow but steady.

What had been talked and dreamed about for years became an official reality when a small crowd gathered in July 1949 at the Owl Camp fog the kickoff of the massive Tillamook Burn effort.

Reforestation Kick-off Ceremonies
Photos by Allan J. de Lay

Gov. Douglas McKay mounted a huge stump used for a podium. He good-naturedly remarked that this was the first time he'd ever made a "stump speech." He predicted The Burn would become a "forest laboratory" for research and experimentation on a pioneering level.

Paul M. Dunn, dean of the School of Forestry, Oregon State University, observed that Oregonians could now look to the future rather than the past. Praising those who had helped put the program across, Dunn singled out Nels Rogers and his vision. Rogers was ill and couldn't attend the ceremony. He died that October.

"It is too bad that a forestry program has to be undertaken in the midst of such desolate surroundings," remarked Edmund Hayes, veteran timber industry leader. "Forestry should start before ever a tree is cut — but that hasn't always been possible. The technology has often been years ahead of its economics. It is virtually impossible to interest people in growing trees as a permanent endeavor until such ventures would repay their costs." Hayes was chairman of the joint committee on forest conservation for the West Coast Lumbermen's Association and the Pacific Northwest Loggers Association.

With a stroke of his pen, Governor McKay signed the bonding papers releasing the funds ($750,000 maximum annually) and officially launched what became the largest single forest rehabilitation attempt in history. Members of the Oregon State Board of Forestry were also on hand: from left, George Spaur, acting state forester; Floyd Hart, Medord, representing West Coast Lumbermen's Association; Leo Hahn, Oregon Wool Growers; Paul Dunn, dean, Oregon State University School of Forestry; H. J. Andrews, regional forester, U.S. Forest Service; E. B. Tanner, president, Oregon Forest Fire Association; J. F. Daggett, Prineville lumberman representing Western Pine Association.

H. J. Andrews, U.S. Forest Service regional forester, signs the documents, while Acting State Forester George Spaur witnesses. A seat on the State Board of Forestry is held for a USFS representative.

During a pause in reforestation ceremonies, Governor McKay relaxed with colleagues and friends amid the wasteland debris. Among them are Walter J. Pearson, state treasurer (*foreground*); George Neuner, attorney general; and Fred Paulus, deputy treasurer.

Governor McKay, in his speech, had high praise for the effective Keep Oregon Green fire-prevention program, founded in the early 1940s. He welcomed the chance to affix a Keep Oregon Green metal placard to his car, aided by Dolores Getty, Garibaldi, 1949 Miss Tillamook County.

The surprise arrival of a helicopter, a rare bird, attracted the crowd. State foresters were already planning to use the whirlybirds for reseeding great portions of the rugged land — the first time choppers would be used in forestry.

A small planting crew demonstrated how this tedious work would be done, in an area near the Wilson River highway *(seen in upper left)*. It was one of the first plantings of seedlings near the Owl Camp. Most planned demonstrations for the kickoff were curtailed because of summer closure in The Burn.

Photo by Ellis Lucia

Rudy Kallander, who headed the rehabilitation program in the early years, sweeps over the mile upon mile of devastation which must be cleaned up before any tree planting can be started. This was once a mighty forest, recalls Glenn French.

Had he lived, Nels Rogers might have taken personal charge of The Burn's rehabilitation. With his death, the task fell to others. R. M. ("Rudy") Kallander assumed the job as rehabilitation director for the State Forestry Department. In early years he coordinated the plans and programs from headquarters in Salem. A career forester, he made regular inspection treks to the region. On one trip, he found this old shovelhead, probably from the original fire. Kallander later left state forestry for the faculty of the OSU forestry school, becoming assistant dean.

When it was certain that, somehow, the Tillamook Burn show would be tackled, John Edward ("Ed") Schroeder was transferred from his Roseburg post to the state's northwest district as chief warden. This was State Forester Nels Rogers' idea; he challenged Schroeder's boast that he could do a better job of fire fighting than those then in charge. Schroeder immediately ran into opposition from people in the area who didn't want state foresters telling them what to do, who threatened foresters and threw rocks at them.

Photo by Ellis Lucia
This was the team that ran the program during the critical years of the Tillamook Burn rehabilitation: *from left*, Curtis Nesheim, in charge of "protection," which meant forest fires; Ed Schroeder, district warden; Bill Phelps, head of land management; and Frank Sargent, in charge of the rehabilitation program. Schroeder later moved up to state forester, taking many of his top aides with him.

Courtesy Oregon Historical Society

Milton R. Mitchell and his wife, Cris, ran the key district headquarters office at Forest Grove, where activity was high all year long after the reforestation program began. They were unique — a husband-and-wife team. Mitchell also served as spokesman with the press, while Cris operated training school for lookouts. She was among the first women lookouts during the manpower shortage days of World War II, well ahead of the women's liberation movement.

Northwest district forestry headquarters at Forest Grove had always been a tiny, makeshift facility. Now it needed to be expanded to meet the demands of the rehabilitation program, including additional staff personnel and much, much more paperwork. Workmen are preparing the basement.

The new building contained ten offices to accommodate the Tillamook Burn. A shop was also built for repairing equipment.

The Owl Camp needed expansion, too. All this activity was an early indication that the huge rehab effort was getting into gear and that it would be more than just signatures on some documents.

Millions of black and bleached snags had to come down, for The Burn must be made fireproof before seedlings could be placed in the ground. The first area tackled was at the summit, adacent to the Owl Camp. Trestles in the background were a part of the railroad salvage effort.

Photo by Running & Cunningham

Lighter, maneuverable power saws were being developed just in time to replace heavy, two-man rigs. Logger-inventor Joe Cox of Portland created an efficient new saw chain after watching woodworms. He tested it on all kinds of wood, including two giant Sequoia trees unhappily felled at Forest Grove.

To fireproof The Burn, foresters needed to create about two hundred miles of firebreaks, some nearly a mile wide, and build about one hundred fifty miles of access roads in the heart of The Burn. Forester Jack Mann kept tab on the progress with a huge wall map.

The entire area, more than 300,000 acres, had to be mapped. Curtis Nesheim, assistant district warden, works out details of the route of a fire corridor in the Coast Range with Charles Moore, fire-break mapper. In reforestation, state foresters used the "block planting" method. Later, helicopters and aerial photography pioneered forestry mapping of The Burn.

Reuben Sullivan dooms another black snag of once-beautiful trees, while Charles Moore estimates its size and the cost of felling. Snags averaged about thirty to the acre.

Snags to come down in initial work for the fire corridors were marked with a large X of yellow paint by George Pritzloff.

Much of the snag-falling work went to private logging outfits in competitive bidding. David McCracken of Seaside and his brother won the first contract to drop 3,751 snags for $2,502. This was less than sixty-seven cents a snag.

The McCracken brothers used new one-man power saws in snag falling, which reduced labor cost. Without the power saw, the Tillamook Burn job might never have been completed. The work was very dangerous; an unknown number were killed and maimed by splintering snags. Hard hats were also being introduced, although not required.

The northwest district had its own snag-falling crews, working in teams of two and three like Everett Rust of Wheeler (*nearest camera*) and Richard Vann of Willamina. Ed Schroeder and his aides were delighted to discover that the new program enabled them to keep personnel throughout the winter, rather than terminating valuable men when the fire season was over. The Burn became a year-around operation.

Even when the snags were down, it was only the beginning. The debris had to be cleaned up in the fire corridors, as Eugene Wooten of Hillsboro is doing. Corridors had to be completely free of debris or they would be ineffective.

One of the unforeseen difficulties of moving ahead with reforestation was that logging outfits refused to give up on salvage. The state owned the land but not the snags, and high prices for logs and lumber found loggers working over debris such as this to squeeze out the last nickel.

A network of roads was built throughout The Burn so that fire-fighting crews could reach an outbreak quickly. This stretch is in the Trask Camp area.

A crew of three could fall as many as seventy snags daily, but the average was around forty, if thickly populated and not over three feet in diameter. Alvin Brown and Al Cissman are dropping this big black one.

All the snags are down in this first planting area near the Owl Camp. The hillside appears fully shorn, but some debris still remains. This block would be the "oldest" new forest in The Burn and would be called Rogers Memorial Forest.

The firebreak corridor would be from six hundred to two thousand feet wide, but the rest of these snags must come down first.

A good road ran up the center of the fire corridor, as another feature of the new protection system. Some 150 miles of roads would be built, but a cynical public was still betting that professional foresters couldn't contain the jinx fires.

Another clean-up method was to burn the valueless debris. So smoke was rising again in the Tillamook Burn — this time hopefully controlled. The results are clear in these pictures.

Gradually the rugged mountain slopes became denuded of snags. Foresters wanted to get them all down, but rising costs forced changes over the years. They had to settle for dropping fire-threatening snags above the ridgetops.

The rehabilitation had been launched none too soon, as the land was looking more like a desert wasteland every day. Only the hunters loved it. The Burn was a great place for deer — which became a problem by feeding on the young seedlings. In autumn, when the vine maple turned, the land was aflame with fall colors.

Photos by Joe Loomis
Just as the tree planting was beginning to get its stride, all of northwestern Oregon was struck by one of the heaviest snowfalls in years, and extreme cold of long duration. At times Timber was literally buried, and buildings collapsed. The historic log railroad station withstood the two-month cold blast, but winter tree planting was at a standstill.

Photos by Ellis Lucia

Even the valleys were hard hit; below-freezing temperatures lasted many weeks, with ice everywhere. Towns looked like Christmas card villages when George Spiesschardt and others brought out their sleighs and cutters as the best way to get around. But progress was nil in the Tillamook Burn.

Chapter Seven

AMID THE RUBBLE

"At times it seemed like we would never get out of the Owl Camp."

Frank Sargent

AT THE OUTSET it appeared that the whole scheme was rather crazy — the idea of replanting a third of a million acres with millions of trees that would someday, perhaps a generation or two hence, again become the great Tillamook woodland of yesteryear. The odds seemed heavily against it, the public had been sold a bill of goods, and even if the little trees took hold, there was always the threat of another fire . . . and another . . . and another . . .

That threat became a reality in the spring and summer of 1951, another so-called "jinx year," when fire broke out at least three times in the Elkhorn drainage and North Fork of the Trask. The first news confirmed the doubting suspicions that reforesting the tinderbox was impossible. It was the same old story of another very bad fire season, with all the buildup toward another Tillamook holocaust.

However, this time it was different. Ed Schroeder and his aides had planned well. Even the loggers were organized, and that wasn't easy. There had been a stockpiling of fire-fighting equipment and trained suppression crews, water storage reservoirs, motorized pumpers, portable pumps, more lookouts, and a new attitude. The rules were being changed, too, for better control of logging and, when necessary, to shut The Burn completely from access by the public.

"When fire breaks out we'll hit it fast, with all we've got," Schroeder pledged.

Thus, the fires of 1951 were contained to 32,700 acres. No green timber and no replanted areas were involved. Thirty million board feet of felled and bucked snags were burned, which was less than half of what was on the ground.

Yet, in the face of a victory that would give a rise of hope for the future, another life was lost. In a fierce September outbreak, again in the Trask area, fire fighter C. E. Gerard, fifty-five, of Tillamook was trapped by flames along the Toll Road and burned to death.

There is little doubt that the great Tillamook fire of 1933 ranks among the foremost disasters of the century along the West Coast. As forest fires go, it was one of the largest when combined forces produced an unbelievable holocaust on the rampage. But how does this huge conflagration compare with other monumental natural disasters — the San Francisco earthquake and fire, eruption of Mount St. Helens, the Vanport flood, the Columbus Day windstorm, the Christmas floods, the Alaska earthquake? It all depends upon your measuring stick: loss of human life, financial loss, area of devastation, wildlife killed, homes, farms and buildings destroyed, whatever . . .

Since 1980, Mount St. Helens often heads the list in the public mind, stemming from its uniqueness, its close proximity to heavy population centers, and from modern electronic journalism. No other disaster in history has received such exposure. For those who delight in mental gymnastics, contemplate how the Tillamook fire might have been covered if reporters had possessed the tools which the media have today.

If human life is used as the common denominator, the Tillamook fire had only one accountable death, and only three in all the fires. This is difficult to accept, but the record stands. The San Francisco earthquake and fire posted 500 dead or missing, Long Beach 117, San Fernando Valley 64, and Alaska 117. The Vanport flood, by some miracle of timing, caused only 15 deaths, although 18,500 were living there. The Columbus Day storm (the Big Blow) resulted in 48 deaths, the 1964 Christmas floods 47, and Mount St. Helens 36 dead and 21 missing. In devastated area, the Tillamook fire blackened over 300,000 acres against St. Helens' 150,000 acres. The Big Blow rampaged for a thousand miles from northern California into British Columbia. Likewise, the Yuletide floods ripped things apart in several states, much the same area as the Big Blow. Vanport's flood was of minor consequence in area, although it wiped out Oregon's second largest town of wartime housing.

In timber loss or potential loss, the Tillamook Burn ranks highest with 11,828,712,000 board feet. Surprisingly, the Big Blow runs a close second with 11,196,816,000 board feet. St. Helens' estimates are far below at about 1,900,000,000 board feet. Other losses were also very staggering. The Tillamook fire wiped out wilderness homes, cabins, logging camps and equipment, backcountry railroads and the Tillamook mainline. But comparisons are difficult between 1933 values and those under today's inflated prices.

The Big Blow wreaked havoc on homes, business districts, schools, airports and farms, $210 million in Oregon and Washington. Nearly 100,000 insurance claims or $24,000,000 were paid. The storm broke at least one outfit, the oldest fire insurance company in Oregon. Two years later the Christmas floods destroyed 12,425 homes, leaving 17,000 homeless. Likewise, St. Helens reaped a broad path of destruction, especially in the Toutle River Valley. Towns and resort communities are still threatened, and the eruption fallout was widespread. And like the Tillamook fires, St. Helens goes on and on, without an end in sight. Unlike the Tillamook, man can do little about the volcano; unless someone figures a way to cap it.

Unhappily, this sprawling wasteland became a tourist attraction, for Oregon visitors had read and heard about it for years. The Oregon State Highway Department posted signs like this one, examined by LaVerne Drake, along Wilson and Sunset highways so there could be no doubt. The Keep Oregon Green people used The Burn as a prime example of carelessness with fire. It also entered the loggers' lingo; any huge forest fire was called "a Tillamook Burn."

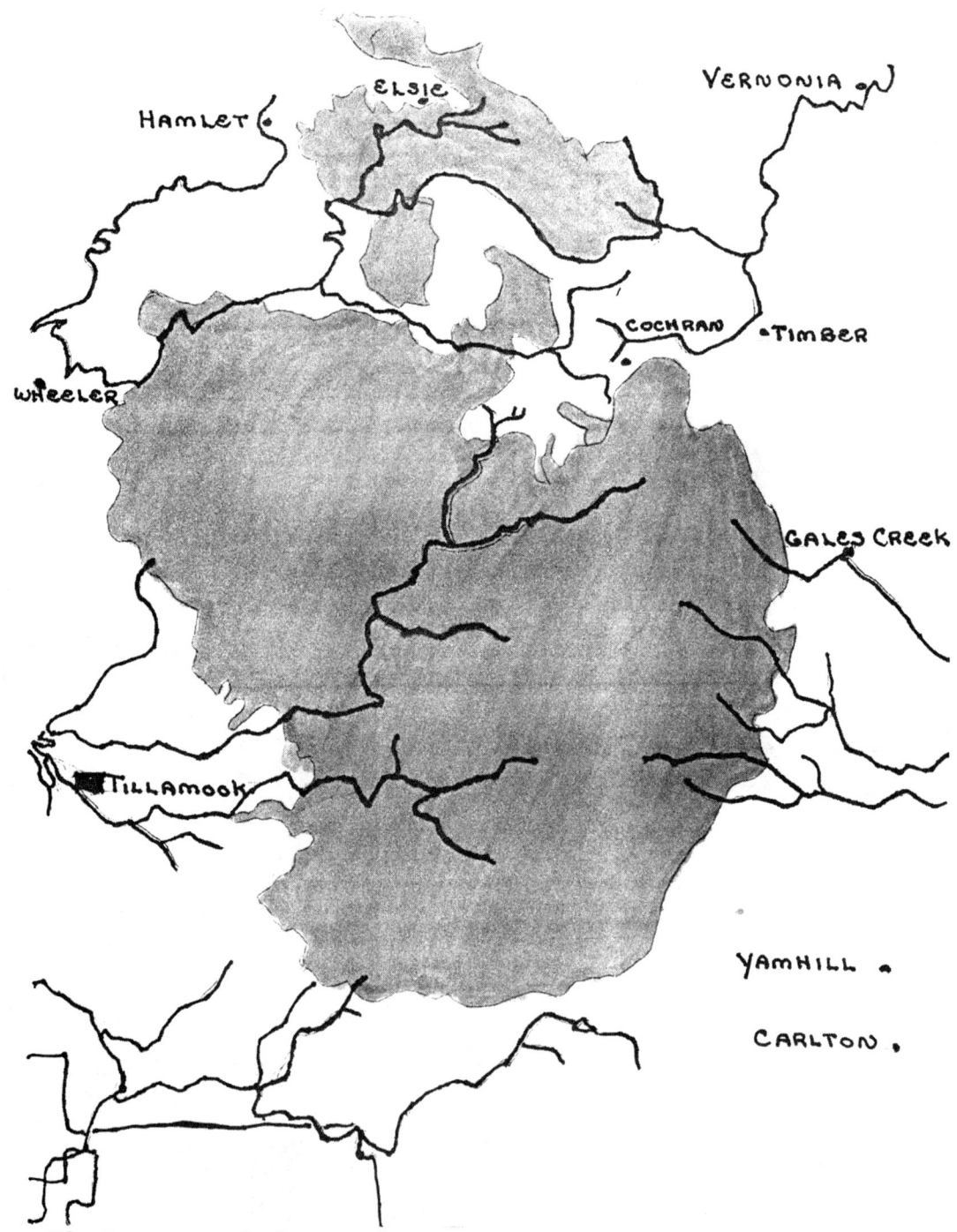

The Burn was indeed tremendous, in very mountainous country. The wasteland from all the fires between 1933 and 1951 is the shaded area, a total of 360,882 acres.

Day after day in season, from fall and through the winter, planting crews moved out to the inglorious task of poking tiny seedlings into the ground. In the beginning, the rehabilitation program cost from $14 to $19 an acre for hand planting.

Seedlings were hard to come by in the first years. Tree nurseries were scattered, and stocks were too low to meet the demands of The Burn. Private forest industry nurseries, pioneered at Nisqually, Washington, furnished 1.3 million trees. Another five hundred thousand came from Washington state sources. The cost was five dollars per thousand. Ed Schroeder (right) examines a planter's seedlings.

Left, above: The hand planting work was slow, tedious, and ofttimes discouraging, with nothing to show. Planters John Toomb *(right)* and John Boggis were part of fourteen-man crews. Brush and fern would hide seedlings for years. Some two million seedlings were set out that first winter.

Right, above: Planter John Boggis could set about 680 trees a day. An acre took 1,260 seedlings at six-foot spacing. Foresters later decided this was too close, and they spread the trees more. This also cut down on the cost.

Photo by Fred Milkie   *Courtesy Weyerhaeuser Co.*

Left: Seedlings were gently placed in the ground with a broad-lipped planting hoe, then the earth was pushed back around it. From then on, like all of forest life, it was left to nature and the elements.

Surveying and mapping became all-important in detailing every section of The Burn. Frank Sargent *(right)*, native of the area, goes over details with Ed Conklin, forest inspector, and Ed Schroeder. Sargent coordinated the rehab program.

The helicopter, like the power saw, was becoming an important forestry machine, being pioneered by eager pilots. Dean Johnson of McMinnville, Oregon, was one. Conceived by Oregon foresters, it was the first time the whirlybird had been used in forestry anywhere. It proved a boon to a program the size of the Tillamook Burn. (See also Chapter IX.)

Other early 'copter outfits wanted to take part. It was a time of experimentation. Hoppers were attached to the sides of the choppers, with funnels to spread the seed. Dale Bever of the Oregon State Forestry Department *(left)* and pilot Tom Hall are loading up.

Two hoppers attached to each side of plane held 110 pounds of seed each. This supply, being loaded by state forestry crewman Lyle Byers for pilot Vern Montgomery of Central Helicopter, Yakima, Washington, will last about ninety minutes. Seed was spread at one-half to three-fourths pound per acre.

One of the first jobs assigned to contracted helicopters was spreading poison seed to take care of rodents. Estimates were about twelve mice per acre, for which Douglas fir seed was "beefsteak." Spreading the poison bait came under fire from wildlife and bird lovers (the words "ecologist" and "environmentalist" were unknown then.) Foresters went ahead, feeling the risk was necessary, since the huge mice population could wipe out the reseeding. The seed was soon treated with aluminum so birds would ignore it. One wonders what the reaction would be today.

The helicopters working from the Owl Camp area proved a valuable tool, although limited by conditions. In the first season of 1949, 15,844 acres were baited for rodent control and 9,700 acres seeded to Douglas fir, at an average of one-third pound per acre. The cost was $4.0645 per acre, at a rate of 60 percent stocking on north slopes and fifty percent on south slopes.

Various experimental hoppers were tested by whirlybird pioneers, and also a variety of spreading systems. This model has rotary spreaders, beneath the plane at lower left. Alan Ahearns, reforestation forester, studies the special equipment. 'Copter owners and pilots seemed as eager to try the work as foresters were to have them.

It would have been impossible to hand-plant all the rugged slopes in such a wide expanse, so the choppers had a prime function. However, the planes also had their drawbacks; sometimes seed just didn't take hold, for puzzling reasons. In those areas, hand-planters moved in. Foresters learned, too, that the altitude from which the seed and seedlings came had much to do with the success of replanting.

Courtesy Forest History Society

One of the spinoffs from the Tillburn reforestation was cone-gathering for seed. Many families — and youngsters, too — found autumn cone picking a profitable venture. The foresters were desperate for the seed. Most unusual entrepreneures were Charles and Mary Anderson, Pacific University students. They established a going business to help him through optometry college. The Andersons had a cone receiving station at their home. He served as field man for the Wood Seed Company. State forestry bought cones directly from him. As an example, in 1951 Anderson paid out $1,300 by mid-September, with some six hundred sacks received from pickers.

Thousands of sacks of cones were gathered by private citizens, who were paid three cents a pound for Douglas fir, four cents for white fir, and ten cents for cedar and hemlock, which was more difficult to gather. A sack of cones brought $2.25 to $2.50.

Courtesy Forest History Society

In the autumn, harvest truckloads of cones arrived at various receiving stations from north of Pe Ell, Washington, to southern Oregon. Bags held about two bushels. Cones were processed at centers like the Wood Seed Company in Salem and the Manning Company in Seattle, major suppliers to the Oregon forestry venture.

Some idea of the size of the annual cone harvest during the early years may be gained from this view of one receiving station. The seed was used not only in The Burn but for reforesting other denuded areas in Oregon.

Courtesy Forest History Society

Courtesy USFS

Cones by the million were cured at main seed plants, later placed in drying tunnels for steaming twenty-four to thirty-six hours, then into churns to remove the seed. Deseeded cones were burned in furnaces.

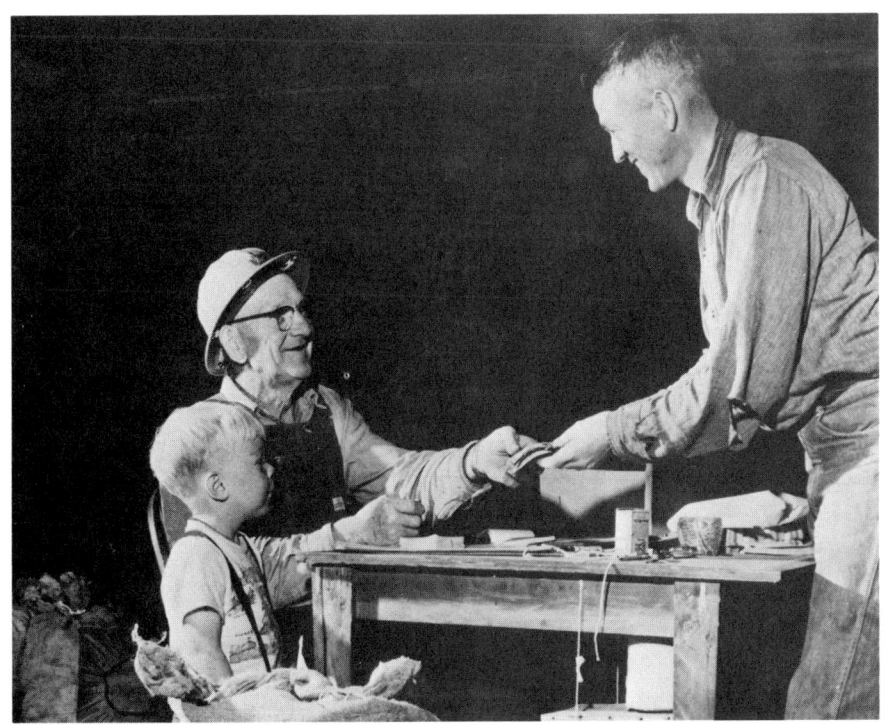

Courtesy Forest History Society

Loggers, farmers, kids, and city folk found the harvest profitable and were a saving force for the Tillamook Burn. One logger and his large family received $286 for four days' work. Average earnings ran around $100 a week.

Courtesy Forest History Society
People collected cones while on outings in the woods. Here is the Bill Stephens family. Harvesting cones was looked upon as a fun thing for a few extra dollars and another contribution by the public toward rehabilitating the big Burn.

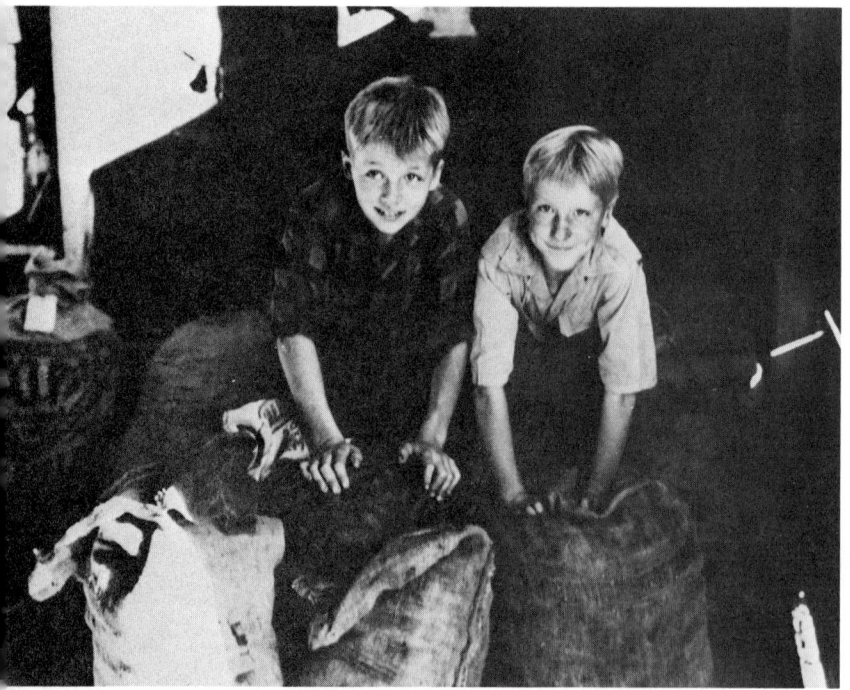

Courtesy Forest History Society
Rambling in the woods on the upper fringes of The Burn, Frankie Jackson and Bobby Sweitzer of Vernonia, Oregon, gathered enough cones to earn three dollars each, which of course brought ready smiles.

Courtesy Oregon Historical Society
In the fall of 1949 friendly competition was staged to choose the "champion cone pickers." The title went to the A. C. Ray family of Vernonia, Oregon, with fifteen bushels a day.

Courtesy OSFD

In 1956 the northwest district established its own cone-picking center, using trusties of the South Fork Camp on the Wilson River. Inmates transferred from the state penitentiary or correctional institution picked about one thousand bushels annually, at a cost of about $1.50 a bushel. At first an attempt was made to sun-dry the cones; then a prune dryer took over the job. State foresters the next year developed their own dryer and seed processing plant. As many as thirteen hundred bushels of Douglas fir cones came from this harvest.

Dale Planer, South Fork superintendent, examines some of the seed processed by trusties

After several years of debate and legislative action, the trusty camp of inmates from the state penitentiary was established in 1951 on the South Fork of the Wilson River. The camp, initially fifty men and later increased to about seventy-five, gave the northwest district a sizeable new reserve force for fire fighting. The trained twenty-man crews were used for battling forest fires throughout Oregon.

South Fork trusties gave the district a source of cheap manpower for road building, snag falling, and tree planting. Inmates were paid one dollar a day, compared with $9.28 a day for hired planters.

Only one cook was on hand when the first trusties arrived, but this would be increased to five as camp occupancy was stepped up. Over the years the camp has proved successful not only for the forest district, but also in the rebuilding of lives among the trusties.

Left: As forestry became more and more an exacting science — pioneered or inspired by the Tillamook Burn — foresters became increasingly selective in picking cones. Industrial and public foresters have endeavored to create better strains of trees, which has led to development of the supertree, so-called for its rapid growth. Stu Welk, assistant rehab program director, northwest district, is posting a tree set aside for research.

Below: Some sections of The Burn became so unbelievably hot in the great blowup of 1933 that reforestation is still impossible. Subsequent fires were equally hot. Rock turned to lava in the 1951 outburst is examined by foresters Doug Burbridge and Curt Nesheim, who points with knife to a molten sample.

Fire patrols and lookouts were strengthened and shifted to increase efficiency. Steel towers such as Kilchis Point replaced the old wooden towers, and lookout life was made more comfortable. (See Chapter IX.)

Below: Thirty-six water-tank reservoirs were strategically spotted throughout the Burn, like hydrants in cities. Frank Sargent, in charge of rehabilitation, checks a newly constructed cedar tank.

The district increased its fleet of pumpers, this one filling up at a reservoir deep in The Burn. In the crucial years of the 1950s and 1960s, the name of the game was to keep fires down, quickly control any outbreaks, and try to prevent flames from reaching the new plantations. In 1949, when the rehabilitation program was launched, seventy-one fires erupted. The following year, into September, this was cut to eleven. But three major outbreaks in 1951 gave everyone a scare.

Left: Year after year the work went ahead at what seemed a snail's pace. Terry Withrow scouts a new tract to be cleared, or perhaps preserved for a future historic hiking trail. To the public, the ghostlike snags became the leading symbol of the Tillamook Burn.

Below: Nevertheless, logging trucks were still a familiar sight. Foresters claimed operators slowed the program by refusing to give up their lands. It seemed a double-barreled case of both helping and hindering the reforestation effort.

Courtesy John Coats

Right: Bill Phelps scrambled over many miles of logs and deadfalls as he handled land management and timber sales during this critical period.

Below: Despite efforts to clean it up, planters were working amid debris on all sides, as Glenn French and Carl Smith are doing. The frustration was that nothing showed for the effort. The seedlings were too small, and for years foresters and the public could only go on faith that something was happening.

Courtesy OSFD
Ellis Lucia Collection

Year after year the planting crews moved out along the rugged slopes of The Burn, often in snow and frigid temperatures and against bone-chilling winds, for winter was the best time for planting. It was inglorious work by state trusty and contract planters. As Frank Sargent said, it seemed to take forever to get out of the Owl Camp. Crews were planting during the administrations of Harry Truman and Dwight Eisenhower, all through the turbulent sixties, big city riots, the Vietnam War, and on into the seventies. In all, 73 million seedlings were planted on 76,234 acres. While the main program was completed in 1973-74, planting goes on as funds become available from state timber revenues.

And the planting goes on . . . and on

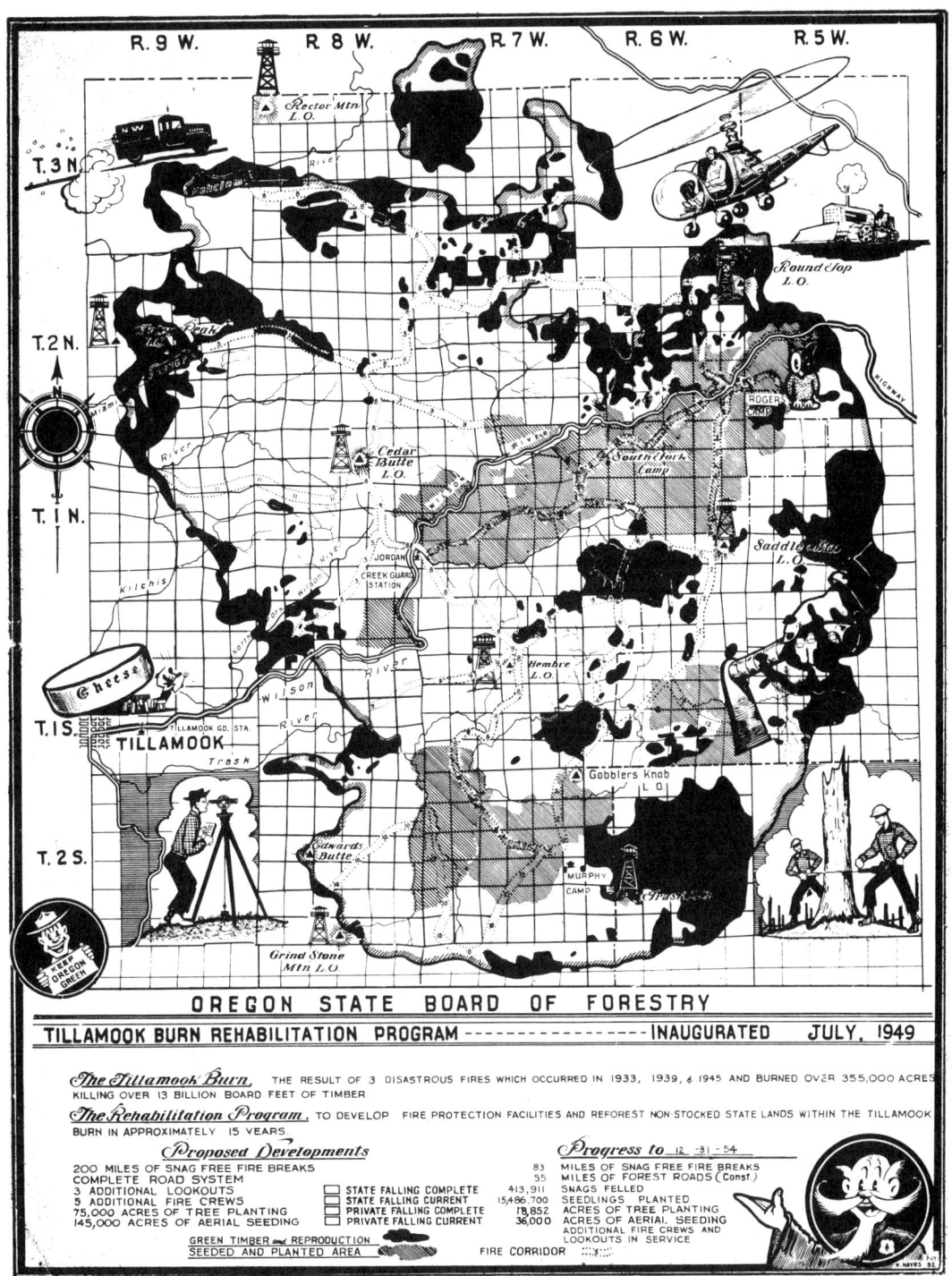

After five years, the Oregon State Forestry Department issued this antimated map, giving the public some idea of what was being accomplished with its money. Lightly shaded areas are those hand planted and seeded from the air. Dark sections, mainly on the fringes, are areas escaping the fire and in green timber, or springing from natural reproduction. Reported were 83 miles of firebreaks, 53 miles of forest roads, 413,911 snags felled, 15,486,700 seedlings planted, 18,852 acres tree planted, and 36,000 acres aerial seeded.

Deep in The Burn the millionth black snag was toppled in 1959, helping to clear 220 miles of snag-free corridors from 1,000 to 4,000 feet wide.

This was the hope for the future, as healthier, faster-growing big trees were developed by the forest products industry and state and federal forest laboratories. Foresters became increasingly fussy about the family lines of the trees and where seed and seedlings were coming from. Some idea of how rapid this new generation of trees could grow is shown here in the year-by-year marking of this tree.

Chapter Eight

A GIANT FOREST LAB

"The vast rehabilitation program will become a veritable laboratory for scientific research and will make an important contribution to American forestry information."

Gov. Douglas McKay

FORESTRY AS A natural science was still in the pioneer stages when the Tillamook Burn program was instigated. There had been state and federal foresters around for decades, but they were looked upon with mutual disrespect by loggers and the public as an interfering nuisance whose primary function was believed to put out forest fires once they had started. The idea that forestry might evolve into something more wasn't considered to any great extent either inside or outside timber circles.

The Tillamook Burn rehabilitation turned things around, forcing new outlooks. The industry was ready, for the nation's supply of trees was running out, smack-dab against the western edge of the continent. In addition, World War II had used up great quantities of the remaining available supply.

The Oregon reforestation effort, therefore, provided the impetus, the place, and the financing for a variety of forest research and experimentation in a heartening spirit of cooperation between private industry and public servants. While a few enlightened lumbermen had attempted reforestation on a small scale and knew that it would come someday, it was still a controversial matter. Only a few years earlier, in 1941 near Montesano, Washington, the nation's first tree farm was dedicated. It was a new idea and the term "tree farm" a new label. Pearl Harbor postponed further progress. However, lumbermen as well as those in forestry knew that little could be done until the fire problem was licked. They were also aware that the public was as much to blame as the loggers. This recognition, and the war, spawned the Keep Green movement, which also began in Washington State.

The Tillamook rehab program brought on all kinds of untried techniques which flowed in many directions — from the forest laboratory at Salem and later Corvallis to the field, or from field to laboratory. Industrial forestry was moving in the same direction. The Burn's activity encouraged timber companies to experiment on their own — or take what was learned in the Tillamook and improve upon it. Because state rehabilitation funds weren't limited to The Burn, experimental projects were launched all around the state under varying conditions, although the heaviest concentration was in northwestern Oregon.

Foresters tried everything, from new planting tools and fire-fighting equipment to unique uses of the helicopter in forestry. Direct seeding, hand planting, snag-falling methods, use of flamethrowers and chemicals, soil analysis, seed gathering, road building, and much more had their beginnings in the Tillamook Burn. It was no wonder that foresters came from around the world "to see what is going on there."

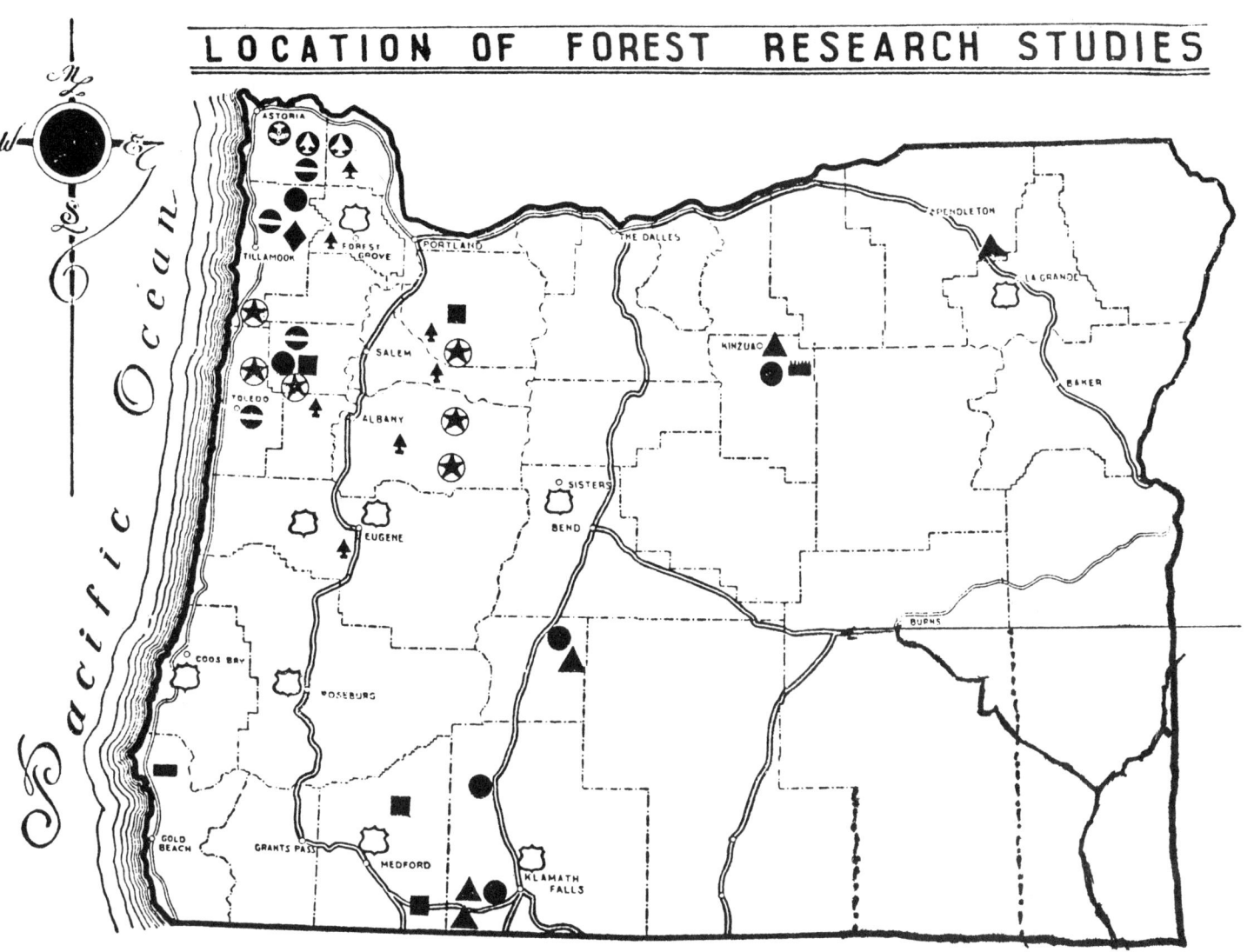

Pioneering forestry techniques were naturally concentrated in the Tillamook Burn Country, but others were scattered throughout the state, as shown on this map. The projects included direct hand seeding, aerial seeding, tree planting, fire-hazard reduction, slash tests, natural regeneration studies, gorse control and tree planting, forest-protection surveys, release of stagnated ponderosa pine stands, roadside strip clearing, second-growth experiments, and forest management studies.

The rodent infestation of The Burn became an early challenge, second only to fire. Hordes of mice consumed the seed. The mountain beaver, or "boomer," was a great threat to tender seedlings. Foresters experimented with poison seed, spread by helicopter. The seed was coated with aluminum to repel birds. Squirrels, chipmunks, and other small animals were virtually gone anyway, destroyed by the many fires and lack of food.

Destruction of tender seedlings by mountain boomers and hares gave rehabilitation foresters many a headache, at times almost on a par with fire. Wire cages were used to protect the young trees until they were large enough to go it alone.

The tiny seedlings were indeed babies, as shown by John B. Woods, Sr. It would take years before the new forest would begin showing above the brush and rubble.

Foresters staked out certain seedlings so they could keep track of their growth. Even before development of the so-called supertree, Douglas firs and Port Orford cedar grew with startling rapidity in the Tillamook Burn.

Growing trees for private and public lands evolved into a huge enterprise in the Pacific Northwest. The Oregon State Forestry Department had maintained a small nursery at Corvallis since the 1920s, but it couldn't begin to meet The Burn's demand. During early years most of the seedlings were supplied from the pioneer Nisqually, Washington, nursery established by the industry. The Burn program, by the very nature of its size and scope, inspired the establishment of many nurseries and, later, seed orchards.

201

Courtesy Weyerhaeuser Co.

Forestry became increasingly an exacting science, with new techniques providing better methods of growing healthy trees. Industrial, private, and public foresters joined in developing new germination, including hand-pollination with protective bags to keep "parent" flowers from being "raped" by wind-borne pollen. Early efforts to develop better lines of trees were pioneered by industrial foresters on lands adjacent to the Tillamook Burn in Clatsop County.

Courtesy Weyerhaeuser Co.

Forestry underwent a full revolution, inspired by the gigantic effort in The Burn. Foresters learned to grow seedlings in capsules, better protecting the root systems. New planting tools were also tested in The Burn, where experimentation would continue for decades.

One of the biggest problems in bringing back the forest was the heavy deer population, which had no intention of keeping out of new plantations. This little orphan, brought to a North Fork fire camp, appears harmless enough, but he spelled trouble to tender young trees. Public sympathy was on the side of the deer.

To study the impact of deer browsing on the replanted areas, and what might be done about it, state foresters teamed with Oregon State Game Commission personnel. A 340-acre tract in the Cedar Creek area east of Tillamook Bay was fenced off and planted in Douglas fir and various kinds of foliage.

The study, which continued for more than a decade, proved beneficial to both game and forestry people. Contained deer averaged below fifty. They were carefully monitored on a year-round basis, both fawns and adult deer, as to their diets and any suffering from malnutrition. Bill Lightfoot *(left)* of Oregon Fish and Wildlife, and Carl Smith of state forestry consider latest findings at the compound.

Deer, like this young fellow being examined by researcher Bill Lightfoot, were marked and their activities and health recorded during the lengthy experiment. Fenced-off sections were built within the compound and planted to various foliage — big leaf maple/snowberry, vine maple /swordfern, red huckleberry/salal, thimbleberry/starflower, bracken fern/ thickleaf lotus, and other varieties — to discover what percentages of Douglas fir could survive. Weather and soil conditions became important. Some fawns and adult deer died from malnutrition.

In a further cooperative effort, the game commission arranged special hunts and also established archery areas, which proved very popular. Foresters knew that public sentiment wouldn't permit any kind of wholesale slaughter of deer, but that additional hunting to keep the population down would be perfectly okay.

Soil in The Burn had taken a beating for decades from extremely hot fires, erosion, sun, wind, rain, and freezing temperatures. The region had five types of forest soil. What would grow where, and how, became of prime concern to soil research foresters like Dr. Chet Youngberg of Oregon State University.

Soil samples were taken from all areas of The Burn to determine the best methods for replanting. Some areas were more suitable to hand-planting, others to aerial seeding. In some sections, natural reseeding might work. Other tracts appeared impossible to replant, even decades after the original holocaust. On a Burn field trip are Lee Hunt, forester, Bureau of Land Management; Paul Lemon, scientist, Soil Conservation Service; and Arlo Krauter, regional forester, Soil Conservation Service.

As light power tools were developed, foresters tested various types of equipment for both planting trees and preparing the ground. Scarification of the soil became an important technique in what became — as predicted — the world's largest tree farm.

Careful mapping of the entire region and extensive surveys were necessary to determine the best method of reforestation. As use of the helicopter and aerial photography developed, foresters found that this accelerated the reforestation and trimmed costs. Such shots as this of one of the first experimental plantings, in 1946 north of Gales Creek, became invaluable as trees began showing in 1950.

The South Fork Camp of prison trusties proved a boon to both the inmates and the reforestation program. The work camp, here taking a lunch break during a fire-training session, provided the northwest district with manpower for year-around rehabilitation work.

As the public and professionals of the timber world streamed into The Burn, the old Owl Camp (now Rogers) continued to be a public amphitheater, as in this 1950 scene. The old stump used in 1948 for the kickoff by Gov. Douglas McKay is at right, behind rostrum.

William ("Bill") Phelps, forester in charge of lands in the Tillamook Burn, discusses the program during a 1950 field trip by the Society of Amercan Foresters. The group was scheduled to return to The Burn in 1983 to view the changes.

Oregon State Board of Forestry members made periodic inspections of The Burn and in 1953 paused for this photograph. Kneeling in front are key foresters of the northwest district who kept the program moving: *from left*, John Woods, Jr., Frank Sargent, Ed Schroeder, and Bill Phelps.

Public officials and private citizens of northwest Oregon were vitally interested in bringing back the region which had so devastated their economy and life-style. Frank Sargent, rehabilitation director, talks to a "county court tour" group in September 1953. On the far right is Lynn S. Cronemiller, state forester at the time of the big fire. M. O. Gardner, Forest Grove city manager, is in the light jacket. Also in the group are Otto Effenberger, M. Helland, and C. Henerys.

Assuming his favorite stance, hands in rear pockets, Frank Sargent explained to a gathering of citizens and local civic leaders that much more had been done than met the eye, since plantings were not yet above the brush and rubble. This tour was through the heart of The Burn, near Saddle Mountain South. Forest Grove, which had much at stake, was well represented. At far left, with Speed Graphic camera, is editor-publisher Hugh McGilvra, who got the program going through his editorials. Lumberman W. W. McCready whose Main Street Yards were known throughout the region, straddles two boards of lumber. Next to him is Walter Vandervelden, veteran fire chief of crack volunteer department, who fought the big fire. Second from far right is M. O. Gardner, city manager. This was typical of key representation, which made such updating tours from all the fringe cities to keep officials abreast of the project.

Professional foresters learned much from the trial-and-error experiments under the widely varied soil, weather, and altitude conditions comprising The Burn. In 1958 professionals from all over Oregon were given an orientation, with Jack Campbell, assistant state forester from Salem *(facing camera)*, conducting the tour.

Alder and other rapidly growing vegetation that crowded out the new generation of conifers were another continual headache for the region's foresters. The hack-and-squirt method of killing the alder was used, but was abandoned in 1982. With demand for firewood, sections were assigned to the public to obtain its winter's fuel.

The northwest district had a transplant bed at the South Fork Camp, being inspected by Larry Fick, district rehabilitation forester. From here, tiny trees would go into the ground in what would be a continual planting program to keep The Burn green and growing.

The timber industry itself, realizing that unless it planned decades ahead there would be scant trees for the future, established its own huge nurseries and greenhouses. Millions upon millions of seedlings in what have become healthier lines are now "homegrown," so to speak, and the acceptable slogan is "timber is a crop."

Courtesy OSFD

At a Burn base camp, a sleek whirlybird approaches for a refill of tree fertilizer for the new forest. The choppers had come a long way as a forestry and logging tool — and what a tool! — since Saddle Mountain (see Chapter IX). Aerial tree feeding was among the latest techniques.

Above: At the base, the 'copter makes ready to hook onto another container. The chopper hopper seems almost as large as the plane and similar to the early space capsule used by astronaut John Glenn.

Left: The whirlybird is up and away to feed this sprawling new forest, just begining to come back. Columbia Helicopters also pioneered aerial logging, using giant choppers from Vietnam War surplus to loft logs from controversial cutting areas in public forests.

Chapter Nine

THE SPECTACULAR 'COPTER LIFT

"That scared the devil out of me. That platform looked awfully small."

Dean Johnson

IN THE LATE 1940s the helicopter was a comparatively new and mysterious flying machine. Many people rated it as largely a plaything for aerial nuts, the latest device passed down from the old aerogyro concept of the 1930s.

But their owners and pilots believed in these strange flying windmills and were eager to demonstrate — often at great risk — what they could do. Among them was a young helicopter pioneer from McMinnville, Oregon, Dean Johnson, who was engaged in the seeding program in the Tillamook Burn.

Foresters were already considering the whirlybirds for a wide variety of uses. The choppers were making headlines nearby in saving lives by picking foolish climbers from bluffs and offshore rocks along the Oregon Coast. The foresters needed to replace a dilapidated lookout building of 1920 vintage, beaten and battered by weather and vandals, atop Saddle Mountain, a towering 3,266-foot peak in a state park southeast of Seaside.

The 3½-mile trail to the top was narrow and steep, much of it chopped from solid rock. Hauling 21,424 pounds of material by pack animals would require much additional work to widen the trail. If men's backs were used, it would take an estimated 430 man-days and 40 days' packing time, plus $5,000 for labor. Yet foresters needed the lookout, a key one in the Tillamook protection system, and they wanted a stout one that couldn't easily be destroyed.

Dean Johnson heard about the problem

and offered to fly the building materials to the top. The foresters took him up on it.

Probably later, Johnson and his co-pilot, Fred Hill of Seattle, secretly wished they'd never heard of Saddle Mountain, for the mission proved a highly dangerous adventure. The hazards were many, ranging from sudden winds and unpredictable air currents to quick fogs and low clouds. The top of the peak, with its thousand-foot dropoff, was narrow and rugged. Fur trappers from the Rockies claimed it was the only peak in the Coast Range worth its salt.

Foresters built a small landing platform and even fashioned a windsock. The chopper worked from the parking lot of this unusual state park to the top of the thin peak, then down again in run after run. Landing at the top was tricky; faces of the pilots dripped perspiration for that platform appeared terribly small, as the landing area of an aircraft carrier from high in the blue. But the return trip was quick, only a couple of minutes, like dropping from on high to the basement in an elevator, whereby hiking the trail would take an hour or more, and nearer two on the ascent.

In all, Johnson and Hill made eighty-five flights without a mishap, although there was a close call in the beginning when a gust of wind nearly swept the chopper over the bluff. The "experiment", which received widespread attention, was the most dramatic of all the programs of this huge forest laboratory. It helped prove the value of the chopper for more than spreading seed. It paved the way for its future use for aerial surveys, photography and mapping, and fire patrols which would eventually reduce the need for numerous lookouts. Conventional planes were also used, often flying out of the Hillsboro airport. Through the years, the helicopters grew larger and more numerous. They became most important to logging and forestry, airlifting timber from the deep woods without having to gouge the surrounding land with skid roads. They were also utilized for aerial fertilizing of the new Tillamook Forest.

Aerial seedings were most successful in the early years of The Burn's reforestation program. The kind of cover, or the lack of it, had much to do with its success. Hand plantings filled in where the choppers failed. The last aerial seeding flights, covering 2,003 acres, came in the 1967–70 seasons, twenty years after the 'copters first took off. In all, more than 97,679 acres were planted by air, with the cost varying from $4.06 to $8.45 per acre. Thirty-six tons of seed were used to turn this land green again.

Photos by Ellis Lucia

The parking lot at the foot of Saddle Mountain was the home base for the helicopter. The peak was often shrouded in fog, even in August.

Bill Holsclaw *(left),* subdistrict warden at Seaside, took charge of the operation. He goes over plans for the first flights with assistant Warren Helm.

Dean Johnson attached special racks to sides of h 'copter for the job. Ken Davidson and Johnson loade the first lumber to be taken to the top. In all, it woul require 85 trips, with an average load of 250 pounds

Left: Grim-faced, Dean Johnson prepares for the takeoff. Johnson knew it was a risky operation, but as a trailblazer he was willing to try. He was later killed when his chopper crashed in another kind of work not connected with forestry.

The forestry crew built a postage-stamp-sized landing platform, fifteen feet square, atop the peak, which was twenty-five by two hundred feet, with a one-thousand-foot dropoff. Lumber from the old lookout was used to build the platform.

The topside crew had radio contact with the landing place far below in the parking lot. By using shortwave equipment, lookout Burt Huggett and builders Arthur Brachmann *(left)* and Don Rust were able to keep the pilot posted on conditions and tell him when the peak was clear of fog and clouds.

Left: While waiting for the fog to clear, Bill Holsclaw hiked up the trail and at the far end of the narrow peak, erected a wind sock to aid Johnson.

Below: At last the peak cleared sufficiently so Johnson was able to make the run. Forester Warren Helm bravely rode along. The ground crew watched tensely as the chopper approached the platform.

Johnson eased his 'copter to the landing platform, which looked like it was shrinking. He later admitted that he was plenty nervous over that first landing.

The racks of lumber, strapped in place, were unloaded as quickly as possible. Motors were kept revved for emergency safety. The chopper was nearly lost on an earlier trip when Pilot Johnson left the cockpit to confer with foresters.

Johnson goes below for another load — this time concrete building blocks (visible in rack). These would have been heavy to pack up that rugged trail. The risky flight frayed nerves; Johnson often emerged wiping sweat from his face. He and his copilot, Fred Hill of Seattle, alternated runs to keep fresh.

Workers unload building blocks, while forester Curt Nesheim scrambles out of way, since Johnson is about to take off again. Unloading was often rushed because of rapidly changing weather conditions on the peak.

Above, left: Warren Helm stacks up the concrete blocks. Work would begin on construction as soon as sufficient supplies arrived. The airlift hauled building tools, sacks of cement, lumber, roofing, a wheelbarrow, excavating equipment, and personal gear — over 3,100 items in all.

Above, right: Pilot Johnson has left the cockpit to confer with forester. He learned this was risky on an early flight, when the plane brakes let go. The chopper nearly went off the platform and over the bluff during a sudden gust of wind. He leaped aboard, revved the motor, and took off just in time to save the equipment — and the project.

Right: In tearing down the old building, Don Rust found the cornerstone from the original structure. The builder had scratched, "Robert Bowman, Jewell, 1920, Clatsop Fire Patrol Association," clearly in the rock. During World War II the building was used as a coastal skywatch.

Foresters designed the new lookout to last. It was erected in about four weeks, the builders living topside in the old shack. The project, another first for the Tillamook Burn rehab program, significantly saved money. The building materials, costing $1,200, were carried for eleven cents a pound — a total cost of $2,300 for the airlift. Eighty-five flights were made over a week's time.

The new outpost in the clouds was built quickly for $4,500, far less than the $10,000-plus for packing materials up the trail. It also proved dramatically the usefulness of helicopters as workhorses in forestry and certainly encouraged the chopper pioneers, designers, and builders to lift their sights to the future.

Chapter Ten

CRIS MITCHELL'S "CLOUD GIRLS"

"I didn't ask for anything. I wanted to prove I was just as good as any man."

Cris Mitchell

DESPITE THE CONTROVERSY that still rages over equal rights for women, it is difficult to believe that until the late 1940s, except during the manpower-short times of World War II, women were unacceptable to "man" the lookouts guarding the nation's forests.

Gradually, however, state and federal foresters began hiring women to serve as fire watchers of the timberlands. A major reason for the breakthrough was Crystal Mitchell, a native of Tillamook, who was well ahead of her time in the matter of women's liberation.

During the war, Cris, a student at the University of Oregon, became one of half a dozen coeds who landed summer jobs as lookouts in 1944. These six young women were pioneers; the following year many more were signed up. It was an important wartime function, for the Japanese were sending their incendiary balloons across the Pacific. Lookouts could also help guard the coast from enemy aircraft. College students found the summer duty ideal for advancing their studies amidst freedom from nerve-wracking jobs in town. However, when the shooting stopped and the GIs came home, the lipstick and powder brigade, as some of the press called them, began to fade away.

Meanwhile, Cris met Milton R. Mitchell during her isolated summer lookout life. He was a dispatcher. They carried on their romance by shortwave radio and visits on his days off.

"It was nice," Cris said. "I got my groceries once a week instead of once a month."

When state forestry took over in northwest Oregon, Mitch and Cris were assigned to run the headquarters office at Forest Grove. They were unique in forestry as a husband-and-wife team. Many lookouts were needed for the fire-ridden Tillamook tinderbox, so an annual training school was established. Cris volunteered to take on the instruction because, she said crisply, "There was no one else who knew anything about it." She also wrote a training manual used statewide.

At first Cris found herself training about seventeen male lookouts, the only woman instructor in the state and perhaps the nation. But soon — and undoubtedly Cris had much to do with it — women were again handling the Tillamook outposts in what became a national trend.

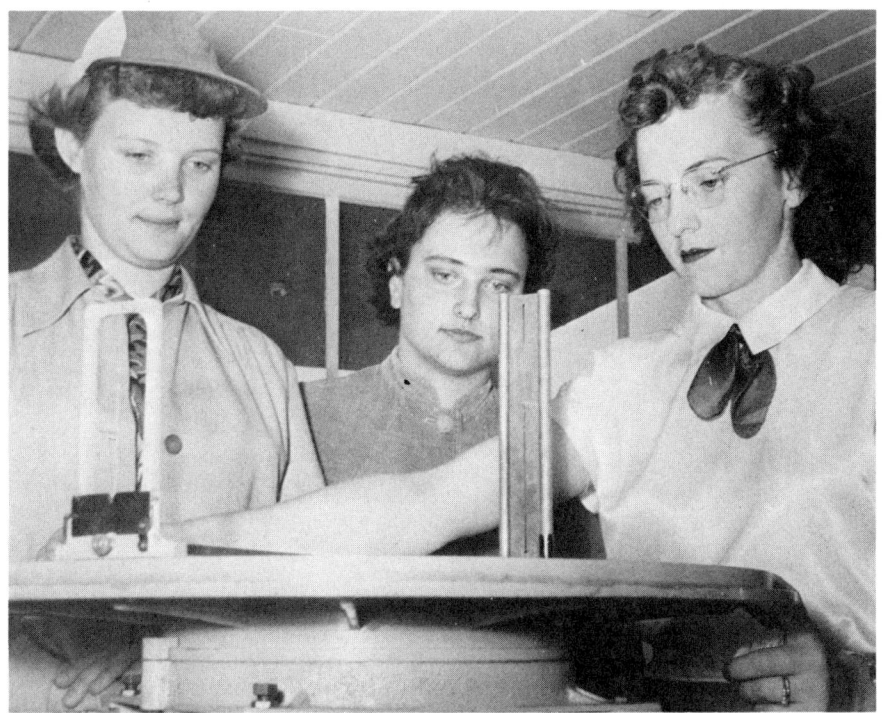

Photos by Ellis Lucia
Cris Mitchell (*right*) took her charges to one of the Tillamook Burn lookouts to acquaint them with the equipment and tell them what lookout life would be like. Many, like Laurel Chambers (*left*) of Oregon City and Dorothy Ostrowski of Portland, were young students. This was their first encounter with a firefinder.

Summer penthouses for the fourteen to seventeen forest lookouts were generally rustic, forty-foot towers like Roundtop in The Burn's heartland. Lookouts were isolated except by radio contact. When storms raged or lightning crackled they had to tough it out and record the strikes.

227

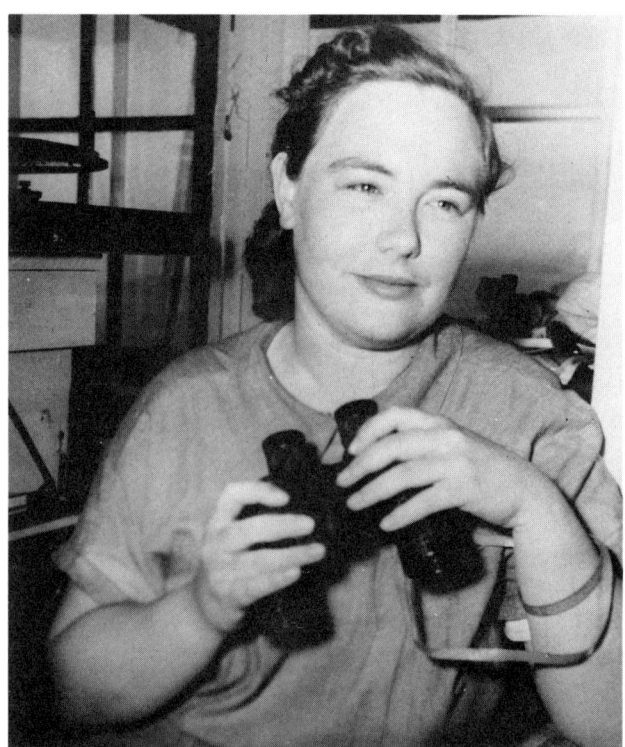

Eleanor Mitchell, a farm girl and no relation to Cris, was assigned the Trask lookout. She brought along her horse and enjoyed the job so well she stayed several seasons. Foresters were amazed to discover that women were more dependable than the men. They were also more self-sufficient. Not all were outdoor types, but they found they could do well without plumbing, hot water, switches, and buttons.

Two city gals, Diann Gillis (*left*) and LaJean Crossett from Portland, signed on for summer duty. They learned that lookouts had to do their own work, including hauling water.

228

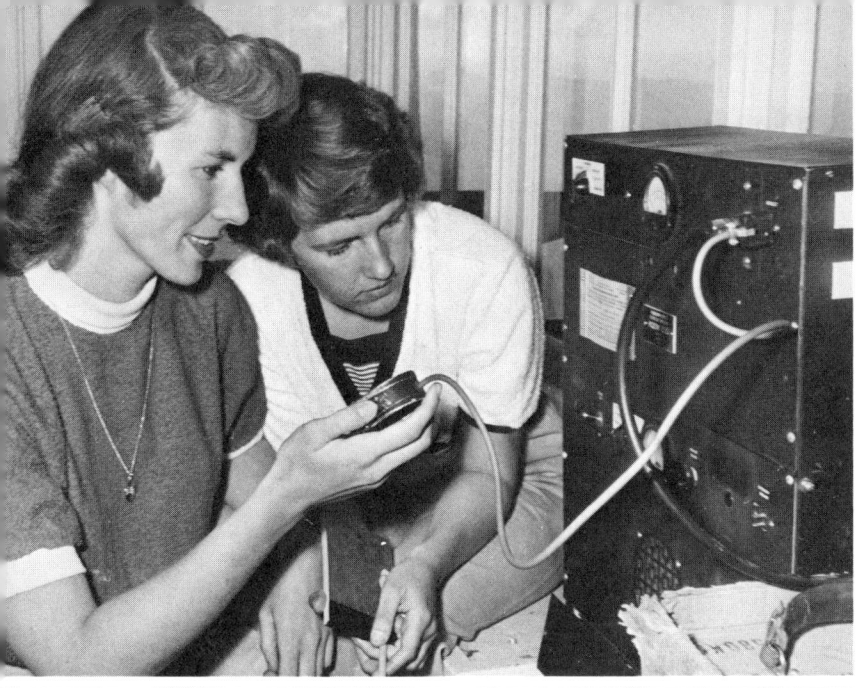

The girls seldom worked in teams, if ever. Diann Gillis *(left)*, an Oregon State University student, was assigned to Roundtop, LaJean Crossett to Buxton. Both attended Cris's lookout school.

Age had nothing to do with being a good lookout. Mrs. Dorothea Hall, wife of a forest warden, brought along her granddaughter Marcele, seven, and also some home comforts, including a television set. TV was just being introduced in Oregon, and the high peaks were good for reception. She'd been doing lookout duty for eleven summers.

Cris Mitchell's lookout sessions grew larger each year and drew applicants from other Oregon forest districts. Owen Knox, dispatcher from Cornelius, Oregon, helped clarify fine points for Ellen Hart of Corvallis.

The women took a lot of kidding at first, but they made good copy for newspapers, magazines, and radio stations. Feature writers dubbed them "cloud girls." Johnny Carpenter, famed radio (and later TV) personality, made the long trek from Portland with an early tape recorder to interview the lady lookouts and their instructor. Said Cris, "The forestry men were very skeptical. We were determined we could be just as good as the men. We were, too."

Treva Harden, daughter of a Christian Church pastor, spent several enjoyable summers in a forest penthouse and found it a much more likeable job than working in a cannery. Attractive, a former candidate for Miss Washington County in the Miss Oregon Pageant, she posed for a series of pictures published nationally, showing what life on a forest lookout was like. Her story was later optioned in Hollywood for a possible TV series.

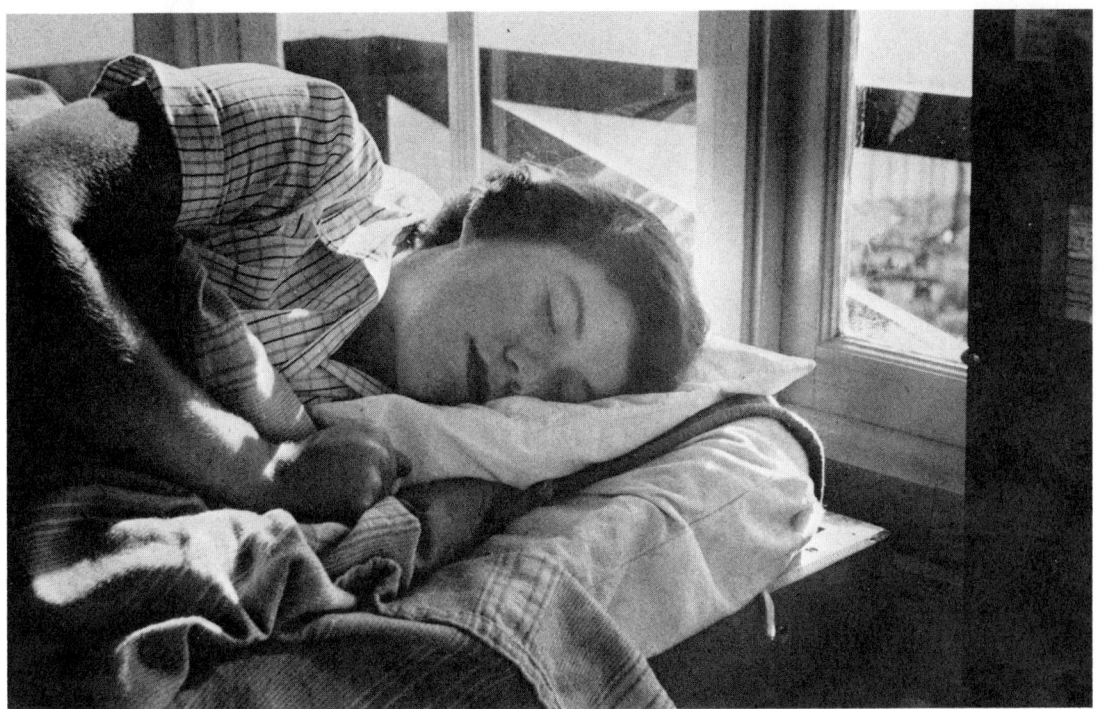

The sun rises early on the high peaks. Roundtop Mountain was 3,015 feet in elevation, with an additional 40-foot tower. Harden found right away she couldn't sleep late; the lookout was all glass, with no drapes or shades.

Every hour Harden must make a full check of her skyline, fifty miles in every direction, then report by radio. In these years of quick, hot fires, The Burn was explosive most of the time.

Lookouts cooked their own meals, usually on a kerosene stove.

You also chopped your own wood . . .

. . . And hauled it topside by rope. Wood was used for heat, as the nights could be chilly.

Right: There was also the little matter of packing water from a spring, one hundred yards down the steep mountainside.

Below: Using a firefinder and triangulation with other lookouts, Treva is able to pinpoint the location of a fire outbreak. During lightning storms lookouts had to record every strike, which, as Treva said, "kept you too busy to be frightened."

Above: No electrical bills here! Oil lamps provided nighttime illumination for reading or studying. "Life up here is wonderful," said Harden. "It's so peaceful. You aren't running around all the time. It sure saves on clothes."

Right: Braiding a rug was another evening diversion. Harden saved her paychecks for college, planned to be a teacher.

Above: Her dog, Freckles, was her only companion. She seldom went "outside" during the summer. Foresters brought her groceries. As safety against intruders, a trapdoor at the top of the stairs could be locked.

Courtesy OSFD

Left: It was a strange forest that lookouts guarded in the Tillamook Burn. But it was most important to keep the fires down and quickly out to bring back the young trees.

The lookout system in the Tillamook Burn began to be phased out as new methods of guarding the forest were adopted. Two or three lookouts are still used there, but most were torn down, favoring plane and ground patrols and aerial infrared photography.

Only a thin trail, barely visible, remains of an important lookout post. It was once a delightful summer occupation, especially for young people, even though the pay was low — around $200 or less. Later the lookouts themselves helped kill the system by demanding higher wages and extra benefits, making the cost prohibitive.

Chapter Eleven

MILL ENDS AND SHADOW-CATCHINGS

"Lucius will undoubtedly go back to Virginia City and tell how he ate in a Tillamook Burn logging camp amid the spruce trees."

Stewart H. Holbrook

THE VAST TILLAMOOK BURN meant many things to people, a large number of whom came from other parts of the world to see the devastation and the all-out attempt to reforest this jagged, mountainous region. For loggers and sawmill operators it was a place of work; for foresters and environmentalists, a land of experimentation, trial, error and achievement.

Visitors arrived by the thousands, some just to drive through, to and from the Oregon Coast, others as part of organized tours. Some braved the backroads on their own, dodging the numerous logging trucks which thundered in dust and mud down to the highways. In autumn the area became a place of rare beauty in the 1950s and early 1960s — on fire again as far as the eye could see, as the vine maple turned brilliant red, orange, and rust-colored. For hunters that season meant something else. During October they hit the region in huge numbers, and at night their campfires festooned the hillsides and ridges with thousands of flickering lights.

Probably the most incongruous visitor to the Tillamook Burn was Lucius Beebe, author, bon vivant, and international gourmet, who wanted to sample logging-camp food. Thanks to his good friend, Stewart Holbrook, Beebe turned an October 1951 day into a time to remember.

Traveling into the Tillamook Burn country, Lucius Beebe was about as far as he could ever get from his world of Boston and New York high society. He knew next-to-nothing about logging and lumbering, and appreciated it even less. Although Beebe now lived in Virginia City, Nevada, the historic old mining camp of the Comstock Lode, the fact was that timber had never received much attention in the legends and tales of his Old West. The Comstock's mining operations had literally stripped the Sierra Nevada range of its trees for underground bracing of the silver mines, but if this entered Beebe's mind, he failed to mention it. The Old West to Lucius was more likely to embrace stagecoaches, railroads, steamcars, and the gas lights, crystal and brocade of the latter half of the 19th century.

On the way to his logging camp luncheon, Beebe, Holbrook and Mrs. Holbrook stopped at the *Washington County News-Times* at Forest Grove to inspect the printing plant. At the time, Beebe was modernizing the shop of the *Territorial Enterprise*, Mark Twain's newspaper, and was publishing an old-style tabloid loaded with barbs, hard-hitting editorials and book reviews, and circulated nationally. He also wrote a weekly column for the *San Francisco Chronicle*, often when in town hanging his derby at the Palace Hotel. Yes, Beebe got his logging camp meal, but it was a disappointment: chicken and dumplings. He showed only scant interest in The Burn, as Holbrook tried to explain it to him. Lucius just wasn't the outdoor type, and wouldn't get out of the car to view the devastation. I have often wondered what the loggers thought of him . . .

Through the decades, the Tillamook Burn spawned a continuing array of anecdotes, tales and sidelights, and will likely always do so, even as a green forest. In 1983, the region observed the fiftieth anniversary of the great fire, and hailed the victory of the new forest. Many newspaper and magazine feature stories were published, together with the reminiscences of people who had fought and lived through the giant holocaust, and had supported with equal vigor efforts to turn the land alive again.

Among the highlights of this half century anniversary was the airing of the number of television documentaries telling the story of the great fire, and of the comeback and hope for the future. A dividend of this effort was the resurrection of old family movie film from private sources and newsreels from the national archives, and also many still photographs. Among the more detailed efforts was a two-part series on a television program called *Northwest Logger;* a brief but concise report by TV historian John Tuttle; and major effort by Channel 10, Portland, for Oregon's network of public broadcasting, in which this author was involved, and on which the show was based in part of material and photos from this book. Called *Greening of the Tillamook*, the half-hour documentary was narrated by Gerry Pratt, Portland TV personality, and written and produced by Judy Peek. Plans were to exhibit it more widely, and it would likely help keep the achievements of the Tillamook Burn from being obliterated by the growing fir trees. The half century anniversary also led, in October 1983, to a national convention of the Society of American Foresters and the Forest History Society, with the Tillamook Burn the theme. It appears that the saga of The Burn will remain alive and well for the future . . .

Ellis Lucia Collection

Lucius Beebe (*right*), who described himself as a Renaissance Man in the 1950s, was living with his partner, Charles Clegg, and Mr. T-Bone at Virginia City, Nevada, the historic silver-boom city. He created a local sensation when he arrived in Portland to see Stewart Holbrook. The Portland logger-author lined up "a day in the woods" with Roy Gould of Diamond Lumber Company. Clegg and the dog didn't go along.

Beebe rolled into town in full regalia aboard his private railroad car, the *Gold Coast*, which he parked at Union Station in Portland. The car was ornately finished in keeping with the Victorian Age, a sharp contrast with a loggers' dining hall.

Ellis Lucia Collection

239

Photo by Herb Alden, Oregon Journal   Ellis Lucia Collection

Stewart Holbrook, who rose from logging camps and timber journals to become one of the nation's leading popular historians, took Beebe to The Burn by automobile. They dressed informally, tieless and wearing Stetsons. Beebe, who was never at a loss for words, bantered that they only owned one tie between them. Yet he admitted to feeling undressed.

W. P. ("Pat") Patterson cooked the high-noon meal for his special guests at the Atlas Logging Company camp. It was chicken and dumplings. This disappointed Beebe, who wanted logger's steak to compare with one he flew north from Virginia City. Mary Watters served the meal.

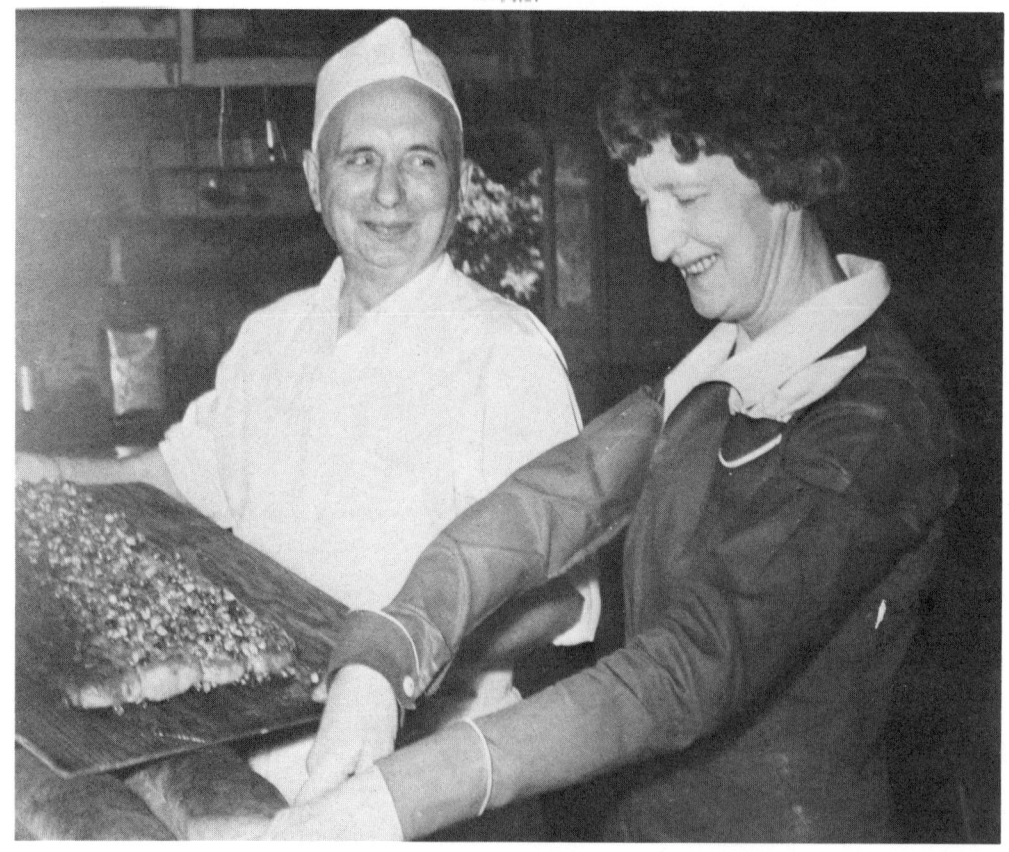

Left, above: Mary Watters had worked as a logging camp waitress for more than thirty years, mainly in the Tillamook country at Cochran, Timber, Mist, Westimber, Saddle Mountain, and Mohler. She and a handful of others broke down the barriers against acceptance of women in the woods.

Right, above: Watters found working in a logging camp far less hectic than in town restaurants. Service was family style; the primary job was keeping the food coming in quantities to hungry loggers like H. T. Olles.

Left: Raising a small flower garden was one of Mary Watters' hobbies. She gained the respect of the loggers, hadn't any regrets, and was only lonely when the loggers went on strike.

Stewart Holbrook wrote much about the Tillamook Burn for national publications, as well as a chapter in *Burning An Empire,* dramatizing the original fire. His contemporary, James Stevens of Seattle, also made periodic trips to The Burn for material for his widely read newspaper column "Out of the Woods." Mrs. Stevens often went along.

Individuals and small bands of people, in and on the fringes of The Burn, were determined to bring the country back. Anglers and hunters clubs had special projects, teaming with the state game commission to restock the streams. George Hoar was among the most active. Here he guides the flow of fingerlings into upper Gales Creek near Consolidated Camp.

Photo by Bob Averill   *Ellis Lucia Collection*

Photo by Bob Averill
George Hoar remembered vividly the great forest and streams thick with trout in his youth. Like many others, Hoar never forgot the tragedy of 1933, which sucked life not only from the woods, but from the streams and rivers.

Photo by Bob Averill
Lester White, local sportsman, gently dumps small trout into upper Gales Creek. While many fish were caught during the annual trout season, numbers also escaped to replenish the streams.

Professional foresters came from near and far to inspect the Tillamook Burn and observe the projects under way there. This was a 1958 tour. Foresters also traveled from other countries, among them Norway, which has had an intensive program and is considered a long-time pacesetter in forestry.

Dead Man's Curve on the Wilson River Highway was the scene of many fatalities, a sharp hairpin overhanging the deep river canyon. At long last engineers and construction crews sliced through the hillside, removing some 300,000 cubic yards of dirt and rock to make the twisting, wheeling route safer.

Photos by Ellis Lucia

Industries connected with The Burn were, by nature, a part of the timber and wood-products scene. But one, near the western mouth of the Sunset Tunnel, was unique to the region and also the Pacific Slope. One thousand feet above sea level, this plant was working on what once had been the bottom of the sea, mining a lightweight aggregate building material from volcanic shale.

Three returning World War II veterans discovered the rich shale deposit and began digging it out. Later, they sold the claim for lack of financial backing to develop it fully. Operators of the big plant dug away at the mountaintop as though it were a gold mine. Geologists and students visited the area, fascinated by shells and other signs of marine life that existed millions of years ago. There were complaints, however, about dust pollution and possible damage to young trees.

Mined by blasting and bulldozing, the gray-colored shale was hauled by a 220-foot conveyor to the top of a giant bin. In ten years about half the mountain was removed, at a rate of four carloads or three hundred yards a day. The crushed, reheated rock was used for building blocks, prestressed beams, and bridge decking.

The raw shale was heated for forty minutes in kilns of more than two thousand degrees, not unlike its volcanic origin. The shale expanded about 25 percent, its weight reduced about half. A sample of the heated "popcorn" shale is held nearest camera. Tillamook Burn shale, expanded and crushed, was turned into building materials, from lightweight blocks to bridge beams in Alaska. The mining operation was later closed and torn down, with the mountain gone.

Ever so slowly fish and wildlife began coming back to the Tillamook streams and hills. This trio along the Wilson is having a field day steelheading.

A sample of the better angling that would come was this fine, prize-winning steelhead caught on the Trask River. It measured thirty-six inches and weighed seventeen pounds, fifteen ounces.

As investment in the new forest became ever greater (even though the trees couldn't yet be seen), foresters of Ed Schroeder's sprawling northwest district became more and more protective. October 1952 was extremely dry at the opening of deer hunting season, so The Burn was closed — amid much gnashing of teeth among the sportsmen. Forester Alex Walter of Gales Creek (*center*) and two trusties from the South Fork Camp erected this large sign to dramatize the closure. Ten days later it rained and the closure was lifted.

Deer and elk created havoc with the new forest. Working with the state game commission, foresters were able to keep herds and deer population down by staging special hunts and issuing more tags. Archery hunting proved very popular, grew into a highly specialized hunting sport, and spawned the cottage industry of making arrows. Bill Powell, McMinnville, Oregon, newsman, paved the way by getting the first deer Robin Hood-style in September 1951 after several deerless seasons. A World War II veteran, Powell gave up hunting with a gun after shots narrowly missed him. He added he'd had enough in the war. Powell also broke the first flying saucer pictures showing machine soaring over a farm near The Burn. The mysterious photos were published world-wide.

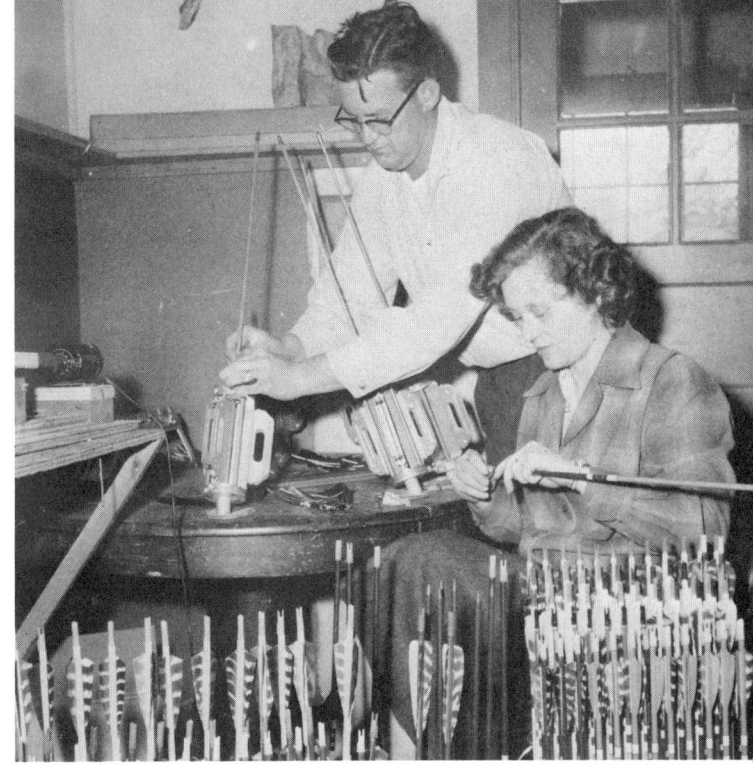

Photo by Don Holm

Elk herds of northwestern Oregon, all but wiped out because of overhunting by early settlers, had been replenished after the turn of the century but were hard hit by the major forest fires. Now again they were on the increase. One of the best known was a herd with a large albino bull leader, often seen along the ridgetops of the Wilson River Highway summit and near the Seaside-Cannon Beach Junction. A winter refuge was established at Jewell, operated by Jim Reeher of that pioneer family.

A November 1951 special elk hunt in The Burn, between the Wilson and Nehalem rivers, proved lucky for this trio. *From left:* Harry Inkley, Wallace Smith, and Al Bowman. They dropped three elk from a herd of about ten, exhibiting antlers with five, six, and seven points.

Bringing in one of the largest bull elks were Lawrence Brabham and his son, Ed. The animal weighed one thousand pounds, with antlers spreading forty-seven inches — nine points on one side, seven on the other. It was downed on the headwaters of the Kilchis River, northeast of Tillamook.

Tillamook Burn timber traveled everywhere, in various forms and dimensions. These two-foot "squares" are bound for Michigan for use in shipyards.

The old Consolidated Camp was converted to a trolley park, using roadbeds built for salvage logging. Trolley cars were collected and refurbished in former Consolidated shops for actual operation.

Photo by Ellis Lucia

Photo by Fritz

During the great years of salvage and reforestation, many championship football teams were fielded by Pacific University and high schools on the fringes of The Burn. Players got in condition during summers "working in the woods." The jobs had double benefits, also helping pay college tuition. The high mark was reached when Paul Stagg began coaching at Pacific, assisted by his famous father, Amos Alonzo Stagg, who traveled north from Stockton, California, to be in on the action.

Photo by Running & Cunningham

Ellis Lucia Collection

Whenever the snow fell heavily, out came the sleighs and cutters that had been stored in barns by rural people. It gave valley areas a New England appearance. Lumberman W. W. ("Bill") McCready found a ride for his family, while George Spiesschaert loaded his big sleigh with happy kids and adults.

Perhaps it was hope for the future, projected by the Tillamook reforestation, but these were generally warm and happy years. This feeling was best exemplified at Forest Grove when the community established a highly successful Gay Nineties festival evolved around barbershop quartets. It was still going strong in the 1980s. Most memorable was the Agony Four Quartet, appropriately representing Oregon State University, where the state Forestry School was located. The foursome traveled to San Francisco by *Shasta Daylight* train for television appearances — a "first" for Northwest entertainers, as TV had not yet reached the region. The festival had been broadcast nationwide for several years via MBS network radio. Quartet member were Bob Day, Bob Blair, Jerry Robison and Joe Einwaller.

Photos by Alan J. de Lay

After television began in Portland, ambitious promoters arranged for an appearance by the Gay Nineties festival on "Wide, Wide World," a popular national live telecast. It was staged at Forest Grove's main intersection where Burn logging trucks had so often dumped their loads. Costumed citizens took part in another first — Oregon's live debut on a nationwide network. The event was memorable, as was the smooth-talking Dave Garroway, who emceed the show. Stumbling on Tualatin Valley, he came up with "Too-uh-la-tin." Somehow it all seemed symbolic of the spirit of the time, projected best by what was happening just over the hills where thousands of eager youngsters were planting trees.

Chapter Twelve

AND THEN CAME THE KIDS . . .

"In 1950 I had no idea it would continue for twenty years and involve 25,000 youths and 2,500 adults. I gaze out at what is now a forest . . . and feel confident we accomplished our original mission: plant trees and grow citizens."

Donald W. Stotler
Portland Public Schools

THEY CAME IN DROVES, in lumbering yellow school buses or silver charters, in caravans of private cars, by the hundreds and by the thousands. They swarmed across the hills and over the ridgetops, pushing through thick underbrush and over the many deadfalls and rotting snags, clutching fistfuls of tiny fir seedlings, wearing outdoor pants and what were called pedal pushers, with determined looks on their young faces.

The kids were from not only the fringe counties of the Tillamook Burn but all over the state of Oregon. They were students from junior high and high school, sometimes college; Girl and Boy Scouts, Camp Fire Girls, church youth organizations, young people's clubs; and from neighborhoods, small towns, and larger cities. Parent-Teacher Associations volunteered as supervisors; state foresters brought the seedlings; businesses, banks, chambers of commerce, the timber industry, logging operators, sheriffs' posses, private donors — all gave freely of their dollars and their time. The West Coast Lumbermen's Association provided much of the impetus, for it was a pet endeavor of WCLA's veteran press representative, Arthur W. Priaulx.

Special tracts were set aside for the various schools and youth groups, with signs to indicate "claims" along the Wilson River and Sunset highways. One particular expedition attracted more than five hundred students from ten or more high schools. This unusual planting effort, which gained national attention, had far-reaching effects. There are many stories of the impact those days in The Burn had on the young people. The one I best remember was of a frustrated young man who was well on the way to becoming a defiant lawbreaker. That day of planting did something to change him — he started thinking about how those baby firs might be alive and growing long after he was gone. As a result, he turned to forestry for a career.

As individuals and as families, out for a picnic or a hike, young people would stop by forestry stations or nurseries to pick up a few trees. Decades later, now middle-aged and with youngsters of their own, they pause beside the highway to look at the green new forest.

To be sure, the student expeditions never got into the deep backcountry. That was left for the professionals and the helicopters. But who would ever say that youth didn't replant the Tillamook Burn?

The hillsides were bare, with snags still showing, when the kids arrived. Schools and youth organizations were assigned tracts which they could call their own.

With fog and chill shrouding the barren ridgetops, hundreds of young people arrive for a planting expedition in The Burn. This was a typical scene in the 1950s and 1960s. While eastern youth rioted in the streets, Oregonians planted trees.

Photo by Allan J. de Lay for WCLA
On a steep hillside, JoAnn Thomas and Marianne Murray of Hebo, Oregon, sink seedlings into the ground. Eight school buses are far below, with Wilson River Highway in the background.

Eager teenagers, supervised by adult volunteers, alight from fleets of buses. Frank Sargent, rehabilitation forester who helped organize many of these expeditions, is seen in hat, third from right.

Getting the platoons of hundreds of energetic youngsters organized wasn't a simple task. Here, they gather for instructions.

This 1954 group is listening to directions. Nearby participating schools included Tillamook, Timber, Forest Grove, Hillsboro, McMinnville, Seaside, Garibaldi, and Astoria on forty dedicated acres. Wilson River and Sunset highway sections were assigned.

Photo by Allan J. de Lay
Frank Sargent, rehabilitation director, lives up to his name by pointing out the area to which this group has been assigned.

Forester Ron England leads another battalion of young planters to its location. They are armed with planting tools and bundles of seedlings.

Countless thousands of trees were planted by the youngsters, who came from around the state. They felt very strongly about reforesting the giant Burn.

Left: Packets of seedlings, protectively wrapped in oil paper, were passed out to youngsters. Glenna Ward of Liberty School, Tillamook, receives hers from forester Glenn French.

Below: Forester Glenn French explains seedling packets to a group of boys. Each packet contained about one hundred trees. Stress was placed on "handling with care."

This eager group got a free ride to their planting area. Most had to hoof it.

Brushy areas didn't stop the kids, who put down trees anywhere they could. Sure, there were bumps, bruises, and scratches, but nobody was seriously injured, beaten up, or raped.

Boys scramble to pick out hodags, a broad-lipped planting tool.

Joe Markee, thirteen, of Liberty School, Tillamook, had difficulty selecting his digger. The forestry department and timber operators furnished planting tools. Seedlings came ofttimes from the Industrial Forestry Association nursery at Nisqually, and from other state and private nurseries as these developed.

How not to use a planting tool was demonstrated, in jest, by this young man.

Fred Staehly, fifteen, of Tillamook was ready to spend the day in The Burn, equipped with hodag and seedling packet.

263

Students scrambled through brush and over deadfalls to plant. Supervisors and sponsors were from service clubs, chambers of commerce, Parent-Teacher Associations, churches, and a wide variety of organizations. In special expeditions, the West Coast Lumbermen's Association handed out medallions, which still rest as keepsakes in dresser drawers and trunks.

Some of the areas were rugged; youngsters got a true taste of what The Burn was all about, contending with black deadfalls in rough terrain.

This group drew a barren, windswept slope, with snags and rubble everywhere.

Forester Burrell Birch shows Pam Johnson, twelve, and Judith Baldwin, thirteen, of Rockaway how to set seedlings gently into the ground so the roots will be right. Youngsters learned much about forestry and conservation before the words "ecology" and "environment" were in their vocabularies.

Ervin Fountain, teacher, supervises one group of girls at tree planting — and also winds up as keeper of coats and sweaters. From left are Lee Ann Wyss, Patricia Witt, and Goldie Davis, all of South Prairie School.

Still they came, even from southern and eastern Oregon, to stick trees into the ravaged ground. The program, lasting decades, gained national attention. James John Grade School, Portland, under the leadership of Ruth Simmons, set a record of twenty-five consecutive years.

For once, anyway, teacher was getting taught! Adolph Berglund, rehabilitation forester from Salem, instructed Mrs. C. Ray Johnson of Tillamook's Liberty Grade School, with an able — and joyful — assist from Jim Walker, fourteen, of Nehalem.

Photo by Allan J. de Lay for WCLA
Stella Cameron and Barbara Britton, from Hebo, worked along a steep hillside south of the Wilson River. It would be several years before their trees would show above the brush.

Students worked in teams. Bonnie Young, thirteen, holds a baby fir ready as Gay Bristol, twelve, works with hodag. Both were Girl Scouts — Bonnie of Yamhill Troop, Gay at Cannon Beach. They were currently from Rockaway.

Merlin Brown, twelve, of Nehalem was a loner, preferring to work by himself. He was very serious about the whole deal.

Gov. Douglas McKay, who served as secretary of interior under President Eisenhower, was on hand one spring to dedicate a memorial tree and plantation to the late Orville R. Miller, lumberman and leader in The Burn reforestation movement. Mrs. Miller and grandchildren participated in the ceremony.

Courtesy Curtis Nesheim

Signs like this near the plantations gave young people a stark lesson in conservation. Foresters and supporters of the youth program believe the indoctrination extended into adult years, often lasting lifetimes. Many schools had special courses.

Courtesy Curtis Nesheim

Areas were specially set aside for school districts, to which they returned annually. Some permanent metal plaques were also established.

The venerable dean of the Keep Green movement, Albert K. Wiesendanger, was always on hand to entertain the kids and stress the importance of the Keep Oregon Green organization.

Kids gather around the "waterhole" before striking out into the brush. Some, like the boy in the background, brought their own canteens.

For more than two decades these scenes were repeated year after year as young people trekked to The Burn. The kids helped substantially to make the forest green again. The idea spread to other denuded areas of the Pacific Northwest and northern California and to municipal parks and waysides. In addition to schools, many youth groups participated and are still doing so, creating another generation of young conservationists, even helping to replant forest devastation near Mount St. Helens.

Photo by Allan J. de Lay for WCLA
A morning of tree planting makes a gal and guy hungry. Young people devoured huge quantities of hot dogs, sandwiches, and milk. Local service clubs, businesses, and industries provided the feed bags.

Old deadfalls became natural resting places when it was chow time.

Rolled blue jeans and pedal pushers were the style of the day, worn in the woods but not to school. This trio must be from the Tillamook area, as indicated by labels on the milk cartons.

After lunch many youngsters went back for another packet of seedlings. Afternoons were more or less free for exploring or following deer trails and logging roads.

Students learned much about forestry and conservation on these field trips. Many schools had special classes on conservation, inspired by the Tillamook Burn experience.

The youth movement to replant devastated areas spread throughout Oregon and to other western states. This expedition was along Oregon's lower Umpqua River.

276

Chapter Thirteen

AT LONG LAST

"We refer to these 350,000 acres now as the Tillamook Forest, but to many Oregonians this will continue to be the Tillamook Burn.... So be it. Call it what you will, it stands as a monument to man's carelessness and at the same time to his dedication. If it continues to remind us to be careful with fire, then the Tillamook Burn will serve us beyond measure."

Gov. Tom McCall

THE BOSS PUBLISHER, Hugh McGilvra of the weekly at Forest Grove, said with excitement in his voice:

"You know, those new trees are beginning to show up out there in The Burn. I suggest you get some pictures and a story."

He seldom ordered, "You do." As his editor, it was up to me how a story was handled.

It was early December 1952 and a beautiful sunny day. Picking up two photogenic high school girls, I headed up the Wilson River Highway, scanning the familiar burned-out landscape. Sure enough, near the summit the dark green of the small Douglas firs was showing above the rusty vine maple and tangled brown brush so familiar to Tillburn folk over the past two decades.

The first horrifying conflagration had happened a little less than twenty years ago. Now the trees were coming back, as if by some miracle, defying the law of averages. In the beginning it wasn't supposed to happen at all, at least not for a century or more. Yet here were the trees, making their debut in areas of the first plantings, not far from Rogers Camp — renamed for the forester who believed more strongly than anyone else that this wild, mountainous, and ravaged land could be brought back.

It would be many more years, another two or three decades, before the Tillamook Burn would truly be green again and the annual autumn spectacle would fade from view. By then, some seventy-three million trees would have been planted and millions more seeded from the air. And the planting has gone on yearly ever since, as funds become available. So have the volunteer efforts by young people.

The girls — Judy Menegat and Shirley Howarth — were excited to see the new trees. They had grown up in the shadow of this great devastation and were inheriting it. I have often wondered how they since felt about that afternoon when they were among the first to view this new forest and whether they ever went back to see how the trees were doing.

The headline above the Page One newspaper photos that week read: "Mustn't Touch For Christmas." These little trees, like the holiday season itself, were a promise and a hope for the future.

Photos by Ellis Lucia

Two high school girls from Forest Grove, Judy Menegat and Shirley Howarth, found new firs reaching for the sky amid the brown fern and vine maple, against the backdrop of many hillside snags yet to come down. It was as though the young trees had appeared overnight, just in time for Christmas 1952 — and they were of tempting size. Foresters worried that overzealous citizens and commercial opportunists might try to make off with the new youngsters, and they kept a close patrol. The first years for the firs, like many forms of wildlife and fish, were harrowing, with many threats to their existence before reaching maturity. Menegat and Howarth found the new forest north of the Wilson River Highway, near the summit, in what were some of the first plantings.

Frank Sargent, who served as rehabilitation director and was a native of the area, found great satisfaction in seeing the new forest make its debut. He could see light at the end of the tunnel and victory over all the ills suffered by the Tillamook Burn.

A needleless tree catches the eye of Frank Sargent and causes him concern. Some of the early plantings placed trees too close together, requiring much thinning. When Ed Schroeder was appointed state forester in 1965, Sargent moved up to district warden. Later, he and others shifted to state headquarters at Salem. Curtis Nesheim, however, went to southern Oregon as district warden. He later became mayor of the historic mining town of Jacksonville.

Ed Schroeder as state forester.

Near huge stumps of the forest of yesteryear, Forester Don Maus checks the progress of young firs. Trees on the slope in the background are ahead of these. This scene was shot in 1958. Chances are these trees will never reach the size of the stump at right, since trees are cut now much earlier, for pulp rather than lumber.

Plantings like this placed trees too close together. In later plantings, seedlings were spaced farther apart. This also saved dollars, since the same number of seedlings covered greater areas.

The years have passed swiftly since those high school girls visited the new forest. The seedlings grew rapidly, as shown dramatically in this wintry scene. Experts proved to be right: The Tillamook was top grade for growing timber.

Now the scene was rapidly changing, especially along the highways, where early plantings were done for a purpose — roadside beautification.

Courtesy Jerry D. Alto, Oregon Historical Society

Many snags were allowed to stand when the program began running low on funds. It was more important to get trees into the ground. The new forest is seen emerging here, in 1958, mile upon mile across this onetime wasteland.

Another view of the Wilson River-Rogers Camp region shows the progress of the new forest in the early 1970s. New techniques, new fire-fighting equipment, and modern forestry make this growing, green wonderland far safer than before 1933.

Among the benefits of this new forest is the return of wildlife like these elk.
Photos by Curtis Nesheim

How the trees have come back is seen in these comparative photos. The first is during the 1955 dedication of Rogers Camp, showing a barren hillside in the background. The second is of Gov. Tom McCall at the rostrum during the 1973 dedication of the Tillamook and Clatsop forests.

These views were taken from the same location in the new Rogers Camp in 1951 and then in 1976. One old-time forester, who knew The Burn well, remarked that he could no longer tell where he was. In right center of 1951 shot, small trees are visible which likely became the big ones twenty-five years later.

Courtesy Jerry D. Alto, Oregon Historical Society

The Quartz Creek Bridge along the Sunset Highway provided another opportunity for comparison. The earlier view was taken in 1940, not long after the second fire of 1939, showing the snag forest. Jerry Alto stood on the same spot to record the change some forty years later. In this and other places, foresters have had trouble with alder pushing out the firs.

From the Hembre lookout site, the scene has been changing. In 1958 the hills, looking west, were barren. Today the new forest is rapidly rising.

Lost Lake is among the natural beauty spots being brought back by the returning trees. Now an Oregon State Forest, The Burn is being developed gradually for recreational use as well as a future timber source.

The logging fire of 1933 started near this place in Gales Creek Canyon. The Tillamook's past is evidenced with markers along both hiking and road tours of The Burn.

In a wayside along the Sunset Highway, the story of the Tillamook Burn is told with pictures and maps, as the new forest rises in the background.

Near Sunset Wayside is a nature trail, also well marked to show comeback of the forest from logging in the prefire woods. Foresters often guide school groups. Young people still plant seedlings in special plots assigned to various schools and/or clubs.

Self-guiding tours of sections of The Burn give visitors a taste of what it was — and is — like in the Tillamook. Guide folders tell the story by number.

One of the most popular car tours of the Tillamook Burn winds through the backcountry from Rogers Camp to the South Fork Camp, where drivers return to the Wilson River Highway. Many landmarks of the past may be seen on the eighteen-mile tour.

The Burn is far different from just a few years ago, when dust from logging trucks still filled the air, frightening motorists who ventured onto back roads. Tours like this from Rogers Camp take visitors through the heart of The Burn, where they see many old landmarks — among them railroad trestles, logging sites, and even the historic wagon road.

Horse trail rides have been developed; this fourteen-mile trek is from Gales Creek Park to Elk Creek Park. Riders pass through areas of black snags, stumps, and deadfalls of bygone years, with the new forest rising. Forester Chuck Anderson leads this group. Trail was developed largely by volunteer labor.

This young rider picks berries and quickly downs them along the way. Because of its proximity to heavily populated areas, The Burn has an unlimited potential for use by outdoor types.

A group of young people, in from a run with their four-wheel-drive vehicles, heads for a dip in the Wilson River. Object of the new forest is multipurpose.

He may not realize it, but this motorbike rider has just jumped a mound on which rests a donkey frame near the old Brown's Camp. Such activity isn't barred, only restricted, in the Tillamook Forest.

Bike riders kick up a dust storm near origin of the 1939 fire, north of Saddle Mountain. Foresters have designated certain areas for bike enthusiasts, feeling that "If we didn't, they'd take off across country and ruin the little trees."

The Wilson and other rivers and streams of this new forest area beckon people all year. Trout anglers are there in summer; in winter the Wilson is a crackerjack steelhead run. Meanwhile, young timber marches up the steep slope to the left.

Typical of the growing number of campsites is this one on the Wilson River. It is nestled amid trees planted by hand as two-year-old seedlings.

Yes, it still rains in the Tillamook Burn, but this foursome of young people — probably native Oregonians — doesn't seem to mind. None of them was alive when the original fire exploded. Today, the younger generation finds it difficult to believe that it ever happened, so rapidly has The Burn turned green again.

Remnants of the old Consolidated Timber Company camp at Glenwood still stand. It is now the site of a streetcar museum, where the public may ride vintage trolleys during the summer over old logging railroad beds. The building in the background is used to store cars and also as a shop where trolleys are refurbished for towns and cities — which put them back on the tracks as tourist attractions. The carbarn is an original and may be found in early photos of Consolidated Camp.

Hagg Lake, west of Stimson's Mill, was developed from an irrigation dam project of recent years. In this area, Stimson's and other contractors logged furiously during salvage years by rail and truck. Not far west of here the last of the big fires broke loose in 1951. Although not within the state forest, it is part of the Tillamook Burn and is administered by Washington County.

Above: Near Elsie, along the Sunset Highway, a private logging buff and hobbyist is building a museum of old timber equipment. Many longtime residents fear that unless such things are preserved, their heritage will be lost to future generations.

Left: This is still "logging country" and will likely flourish again as sections of the Tillamook Forest are harvested. At Oney's restaurant and tavern, long a loggers' hangout, a large museum of pictures and artifacts has been developed. It is also the locale for loggers' reunions.

With costs of other kinds of heating on the rise, and with continued energy crises, Oregonians are again turning to wood. The timing is right, for foresters have had trouble controlling the growth of alder and other hardwoods that crowd out the young trees of the new Tillamook Forest. Foresters assign tracts and issue permits for woodcutting — and in the fall the public lines up.

In the Oregon of yesteryear, the sound of the woodcutter's saw signaled that fall was near, winter coming. Now that sound is back, as citizens haul wood from The Burn at ten dollars a permit.

The tree planting goes on, even though the main reforestation program was completed in 1973. As funds become available, seedlings are placed in the ground each year, in barren areas where trees have failed to grow or where animals have feasted heavily.

Courtesy Oregon State Department of Forestry

The Tillamook Burn became productive again with new-growth timber in late June 1983, when the first logging took place in the restored forest south of Rogers Camp. The "bigstick thinning" of commercial timber was in one of the early-planted areas. Ken Risseeuw, Sheridan logging contractor, won the bid at $75 per thousand board feet or 470,000 board feet at $35,000. The historic first logs, signifying victory over disaster, were processed by the Willamina Lumber Company seventy miles away.

Thus the dream of Nels Rogers, forester and visionary, has come true, thirty years after his death. With stubborn tenacity, the native of Tillamook Burn Country stood alone at times in believing that the great wasteland could be returned to full life. This painting of Rogers, by artist Stan Galli, hangs in the office of the Oregon state forester, depicting what Rogers conceived and what he planned. His legacy grew and gradually unfolded — maybe more rapidly than he visualized but not fast enough for him to live to see it. He passed the torch to others. Perhaps Ed Schroeder, whom Rogers himself brought to The Burn, was thinking of Rogers when he said: "It is seldom in a man's lifetime that he is able to see something like this happen. It makes a fellow feel pretty proud to have been a part of it." The Rogers Memorial Forest extends a short distance from the summit at Rogers Camp. In a way, the entire Tillamook Forest is his memorial.

TILLAMOOK BURN SUMMARY

(Based on Statistics Compiled by
Oregon State Department of Forestry)

	Board Feet	Acres
1933 (Tillamook)		
Perimeter area		261,222
Unburned area within perimeter		21,527
Burned area		239,695*
Timber killed	11,828,712,000	
*Revised from original 311,000 acres		
1939 (Saddle Mountain)		
Perimeter area		209,690
Unburned area within perimeter		19,030
Burned area		189,660
Timber killed	834,220,000	
Additional area burned over		
Green timber		28,180
Logged over		6,384
Previously burned by other fires		15,527
1945 (Wilson River, Salmonberry)		
Perimeter area		182,370
Unburned area within perimeter		2,240
Burned area		180,130
Timber killed	439,985,000	
Additional area burned over		
Green timber		12,571
Logged over		36,211
Previously burned by other fires		10,899
Hemlock looper (insect) kill		5,469
1951 (North Fork — Elkhorn)		
Burned area		32,700
(Total area was burned by 1933 and 1939 fires)		
Green timber or reforested areas burned		None
Felled and bucked snags burned (less than ½ destroyed)	30,000,000	
Additional area burned over		None
Totals: All Four Fires		
Perimeter area		360,882
Unburned area within perimeter		5,946
Burned area		354,936
Timber killed	13,102,917,000	
(Enough timber for over one million five-room homes)		

Loss of life:
   Human 3
   Birds, animals .... Unestimated millions
   Additional deaths from salvage and snag falling not tabulated.

SALVAGE 1934-1955
Fire-Killed Timber

Value (1933) if not burned (Calculated use over 20 years)	$442.4 million
Stumpage value (11.8 billion bf)	$ 90.0 million
Wages for processing trees	$350.0 million
Taxes from forest landowners	$ 2.4 million
Pre-fire timber value, 1939 and 1945 fires	$ 20.2 million
Stumpage value (1.3 billion bf)	$ 4.2 million
Wages	$ 16.0 million
Fire-killed timber volume estimated	13.1 billion bf
1934–1948 salvage	4.0 billion bf
1949–1955 salvage	3.5 billion bf
Total	7.5 billion bf
Value recovered 1934–1948	$ 27,420,881
Value recovered 1949–1955	$ 72,361,076
Total recovered	$ 99,781,957
Consolidated Timber expenditures:	
Railroad construction	$ 1,500,000
Railroad rolling stock, equipment	$ 1,250,000
Truck roads	$ 800,000

REFORESTATION 1948-1973

Snags felled	1.5 million
Snag-free corridors built (1,000 - 4,000 ft. wide)	220 miles
"Problem area"	500,000 acres
Total Burn area	365,000 acres
Access road construction (30-minute access)	165 miles
Road construction 1934–1955	2,800 miles
Cedar water tanks construction	36
Lookouts — Northwest district	14–17
Wages	$90 - $200 per mo.
Suppression crews	3 crews, 5 - 8 men
	20-man crew, S. Fork Camp
Expenditure:	
State bond issue, 1948	$10,500,000
Limit per year	$750,000
Direct cost prior 1973	$12,000,000
(1974 — Financing for future rehabilitation from revenues, state forest lands)	
Replanting	325 square miles
Hand-planting	76,234 acres
Seedlings	72–73 million
Cost	Approx. $82 per thousand
Hand-planting wages:	
1956	$1.30 hr.
	$12.00 day
1972	$2.85 hr.
	$25.00 day
Cost per acre (early years)	$25.00
Cost per acre (later years)	$75.00
Helicopter seeding 1949–1970	97,679 acres
Amount of seed (½ - ¾ lb. per acre)	36 tons
Last aerial seedings 1967–70	2,003 acres
Cost per acre	$4.06 - $8.45
Cost of own seed	$3.00 - $4.00 lb.

Site preparation:
   1957–1973 .... 68,635 acres treated with chemicals or mechanically to make room for new forest
   1974–1983 .... Release of conifer stands threatened by competing vegetation

Seedling spacing:
   Beginning .... 6 x 6 feet
   1st revised .... 6 x 8 feet
   2nd revision .... 10 x 10 feet
   3rd revision .... 12 x 12 feet

Last plantings, 1972–73:
   Acres 4,000
   Number of seedlings .... 2 million
   Manpower .... 120 men (12 crews, 10 men each)

South Fork inmate camp (established 1951):
   Original work force 50
   1956 66
   1960 75
   Current .... Varies
   Special trained fire crew (Used also for
     snag falling, road building) 20

Management:
   Pre-commercial thinning:
     1968–1973 .... 8,376 acres
     1974–1980 .... 5,351 acres
   Fertilization:
     1978–1980 .... 6,300 acres

NEW TILLAMOOK FOREST

Size (Tillamook and Washington Counties) .... 364,000 acres
Investment .... $12 million
                                                          24 years
Revenue return .... $2 billion from initial crop based on 1979 stumpage prices
Revenue in 1980s est. (Revenue to increase
   estimated four times by 2015) $500,000
Public facilities .... 271 acres
   Parks 11
   Campsites 333
     Other developments: Hiking and horse trails, swimming areas, boat launchings, fishing places, motor bike areas, viewpoints, berrypicking areas, hunting, general outdoor recreation facilities.

Planned harvests 1980s .... 950-acre thinning of 32–35 year-old trees on site of original plantings
Annual cut .... 9 million cubic feet
By year 2015 .... 31 million cubic feet annually (oldest plantings 30–35 years)
June 1983, first commercial thinning by
   Ken Risseeuw, Sheridan Oregon, logger .... 470,000 bf on 114 acres at $75 per 1,000 bf
                                                          Total bid ... $35,000

(Area south of Rogers Camp. First tree felled,
   35-year-old Douglas fir, 25 inches in diameter.)
(Harvest schedules based on economic conditions and timber needs)

BIBLIOGRAPHY

Most of the facts and anecdotes contained in this book are drawn from personal experience and observation, and are based on my writings in newspapers and magazines of past years. Many of these articles appeared in the *Washington County News-Times*, the *Northwest Magazine* of *The Oregonian*, the *Oregon Journal* news and feature sections, and subsequently also in the *New York Times, Washington Post* (reprinted in the *Congressional Record*), *National Parent-Teacher*, *The Nation*, and many other national and regional publications.

I relied heavily on my own extensive files collected through the years (including raw notes from reporting days) and also upon early maps, tape-recorded interviews, negatives and prints, clippings and tearsheets accumulated and preserved under various topics of The Burn story. The extensive files of the Oregon State Forestry Department were also checked, and foresters who shaped the reforestation program — among them Ed Schroeder, Frank Sargent, Bill Phelps and Curtis Nesheim — were frequently consulted on some of the fine points.

The following books were used:

Abdill, George. *This Was Railroading*. Seattle: Superior Publishing Company, 1958.

Andrews, Ralph W. *This Was Logging*. Seattle: Superior Publishing Company, 1954.

———. *This Was Sawmilling*. Seattle: Superior Publishing Company, 1957.

Cavalier, Julian. *Classic American Railroad Stations*. San Diego: A. S. Barnes & Company, 1980.

Culp, Edwin D. *Oregon The Way It Was*. Caldwell, Idaho: The Caxton Printers, 1981.

Holbrook, Stewart H. *Burning an Empire: The Story of American Forest Fires*. New York: The Macmillan Company, 1943.

Kemp, J. Larry. *Epitaph for the Giants: The Story of the Tillamook Burn*. Beaverton, Oregon: Touchstone Press, 1967.

Lucia, Ellis. *Head Rig: Story of the West Coast Lumber Industry*. Portland, Oregon: Overland West Press, 1965.

———. *The Big Woods: Logging and Lumbering in the Pacific Northwest*. New York: Doubleday & Company, 1975.

Luebke, Helen Reeher. *Pioneers of the Wilson River Stage Road*. Forest Grove, Oregon: Privately published as a family history.

Miller, Emma Gene. *Clatsop County, Oregon: Its History, Legends and Industries*. Portland, Oregon: Binfords & Mort, 1958.

Oregon State Game Commission. *Research Report #3: Black-Tailed Deer Population & Douglas Fir Reforestation in the Tillamook Burn*. Published at Portland, Oregon.

Pierre, Joseph. *When Timber Stood Tall*. Seattle: Superior Publishing Company, 1979.

Reeher, Mildred S. *The Home Within the Wilderness*. Forest Grove, Oregon: Self-published, 1954.

Tillamook Pioneer Association. *Tillamook Memories*. Tillamook, Oregon, 1972.